Traini

Goa... scorers

103 Drills to Improve Your Team's Finishing Ability

by

Michael Beale

Published by
WORLD CLASS COACHING

First published January, 2008 by
WORLD CLASS COACHING 15004 Buena Vista Drive, Leawood, KS 66224
(913) 402-0030

ISBN 0-9788936-8-2

Author - Michael Beale

Front Cover Picture - Wayne Rooney while playing for England

Cover Design by P2 Creative Solutions

Published by
WORLD CLASS COACHING

Introduction

Question – do you remember the first time you scored a goal in a real soccer match?

Can you remember how it felt? The confidence it gave you or how you celebrated the goal?

"I certainly can. I was seven years old and playing for Vista football club u9's at white foot lane playing fields. Our team had a corner kick, I was playing on the left and ran towards my teammate looking to receive a pass in-line with the corner of the 18yd box. My team-mate (I cannot recall his name) passed the ball in my direction, I ran towards the ball and I smashed it first time, high towards the goal. I then watched as the ball sailed over the goalkeepers head and into the goal.

Was it a cross or was it a shot? Who cares, I had just scored my first goal. I remember freezing for a minute but then my body wanted to burst so I just ran as fast as I could in no particular direction. My dad was also excited and I think he did the same.

I will never forget that day, I can still see and feel it when I close my eyes. That day, I fell in love with football.

The practices in this book are designed to inspire your players to score goals and experience this special feeling as much as possible. The practices are realistic to the real game in intensity, range of techniques/skills used, pressure of the opponent, decision making and choices on the ball.

Soccer has many rules but one aim. That aim is to score more goals than your opponent and win the game. No matter what level you play, what age, what tactics you employ, this aim will never change. Soccer is a simple game that is often made difficult by players but more regularly by coaches.

If the aim of soccer is to score more goals than your opponent then the guideline to all coaches is simple. we must develop an attitude and desire within our players to attack freely in order to create and score goals.

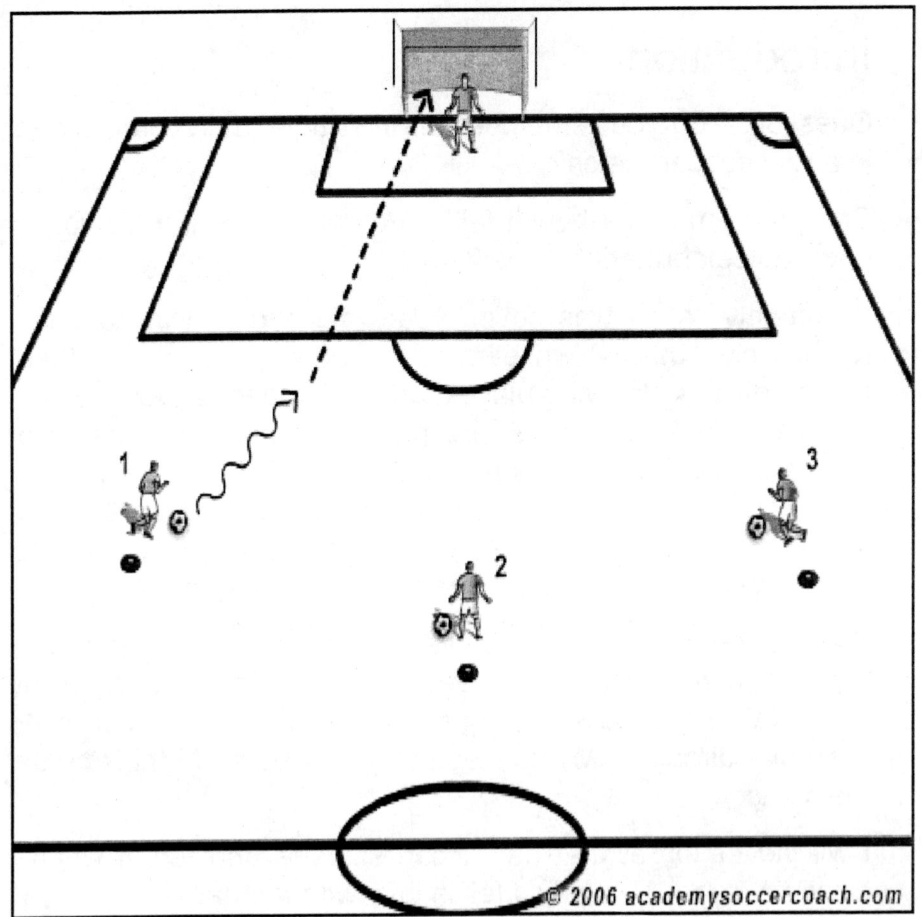

<u>Practice 1</u>

Player 1 dribbles and shoots at goal
player 2 plays a one-two with player 1 and shoots
Player 3 dribbles past a "passive" player 2 and shoots

<u>Practice 2</u>

Player 1 dribbles and shoots
Player 2 plays a one-two with player 1 and shoots
Player 3 dribbles and attacks in a 1v1 against player 2 who attempts to defend

<u>Practice 3</u>

Player 1 dribbles and shoots
Player 2 dribbles and attacks in a 1v1 against player 1
Player 3 combines with player 1 in a 2v1 situation against player 2

<u>Practice 4</u>

Player 1 dribbles and shoots
Player 2 dribbles and attacks in a 1v1 against player 1
Player 3 makes a choice of which team mate he would like and passes into that player to make a 2v1 situation

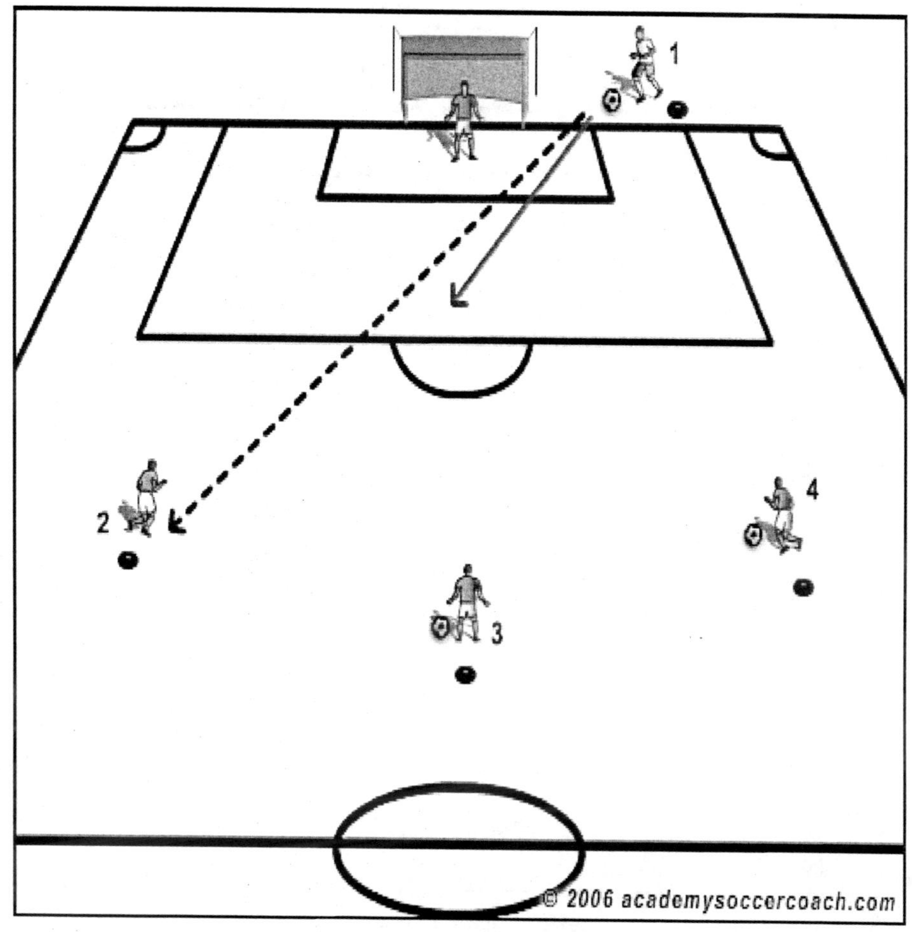

<u>Practice 6</u>

Player 1 passes to player 2 and defends 1v1
Player 3 and player 2 play a 2v1 against player 1
Player 4 dribbles and crosses for players 2 and 3 who attempt to lose player 1 and score.

<u>Practice 7</u>

Player 1 passes to a player of their choice and then runs to defend 1v1
The player chosen now selects a team mate for a 2v1 against player 1
The last player remaining then dribbles into the area and combines with player 1 in a 2v2 game

<u>Practice 8</u>

Player 1 runs out to the edge of the box, receives a pass from player 3 and turns to shoot
Immediately player 4 passes to player 3, player 3 then switches out wide to player 2
Player 2 now dribbles and crosses for players 3 and 4
Players 3 and 4 must lose the defender (player 1) and attempt to score

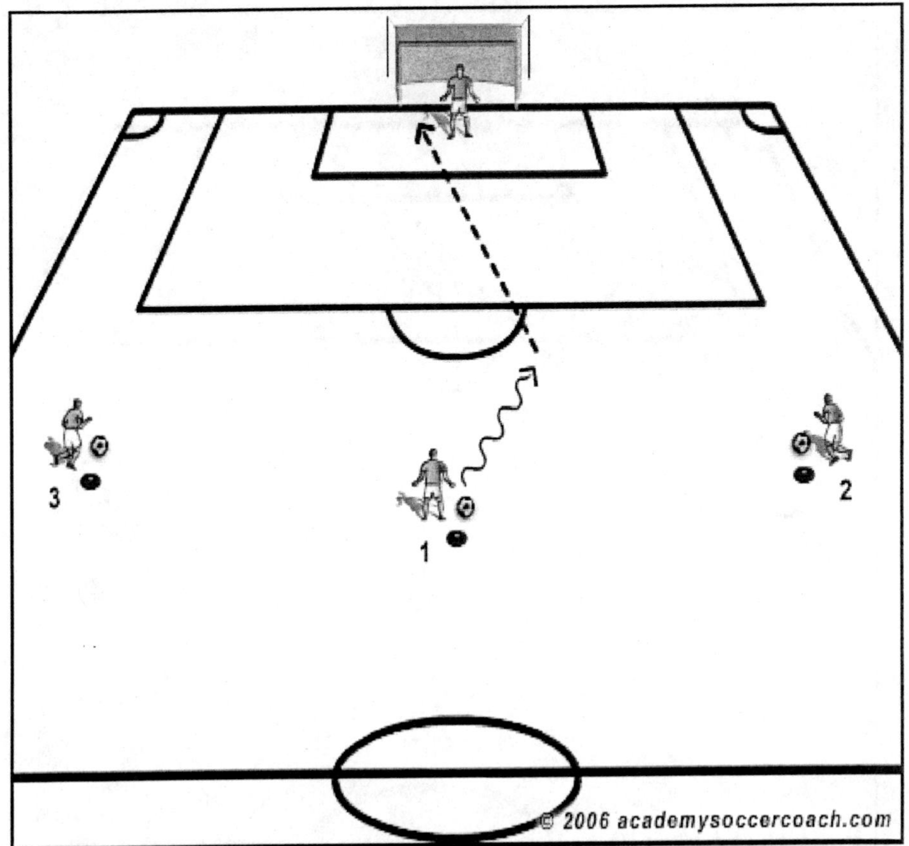

<u>Same process for all practices</u>
Player 1 dribbles and shoots at goal
Player 1 now turns and makes a choice of which player to combine with
The player chosen passes to player 1 and runs inside to receive a return pass

Practice 9

The ball is then passed out wide to the opposite player
Player 1 and his chosen team mate now run into the penalty box and attempt to score from the cross

Practice 10

The ball is then passed out wide to the opposite player
Player 1 reacts and becomes a defender against the two other players

Practice 11

The player makes a through pass for the opposite player to run and shoot at goal

Practice 12

The player makes a through pass for the opposite player to run and shoot at goal
Player 1 now becomes a defender and attempts to stop the player scoring

Practice 13

The player chosen passes to player 1 and runs out wide to receive a return pass
Now the player crosses for the opposite player to run into the box and score

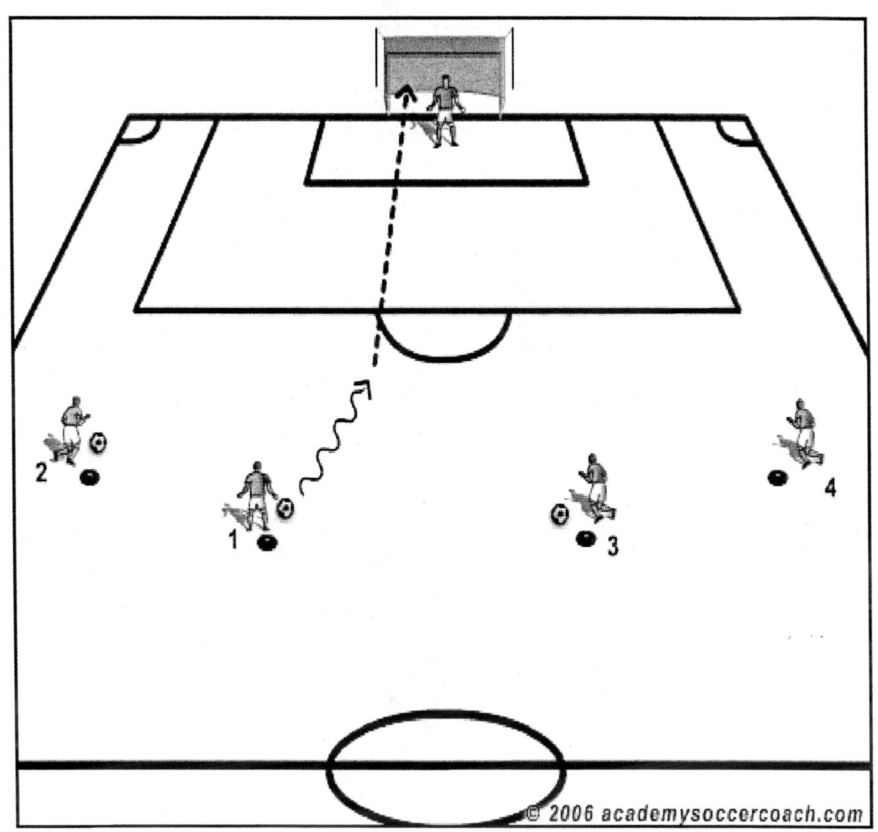

<u>Practice 14</u>

Player 1 dribbles and shoots at goal
Player 2 passes to player 1 and runs out wide to receive a return pass
Player 2 crosses for player 4 to run into the box and attempt to score
Player 3 dribbles into the area to attack 1v1 against player 4

<u>Practice 15</u>

Same as above but now player 2 and player 4 defend 2v1 against player 3

<u>Practice 16</u>

Same as above but now player 3 combines with player 1 to make a 2v2 against players 2 and 4

<u>Practice 17</u>

Player 2 dribbles and crosses for player 3
Player 4 dribbles and crosses for player 1
The coach now passes to player 2 or player 4
A 2v2 game commences with players 2 and 4 against players 1 and 3

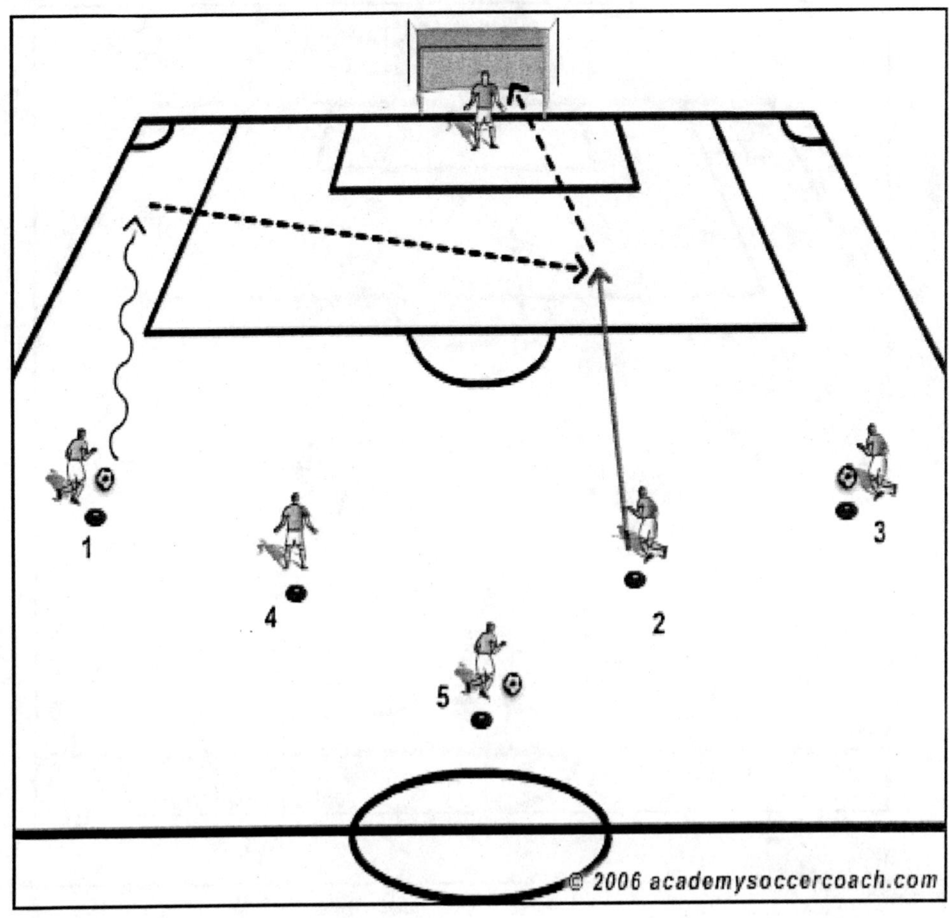

<u>Practice 18</u>

Player 1 dribbles and crosses for player 2
Player 3 dribbles and crosses for player 4
Now player 5 dribbles into the pitch and makes a 3v2 game with players 1 and 2 against 3 and 4

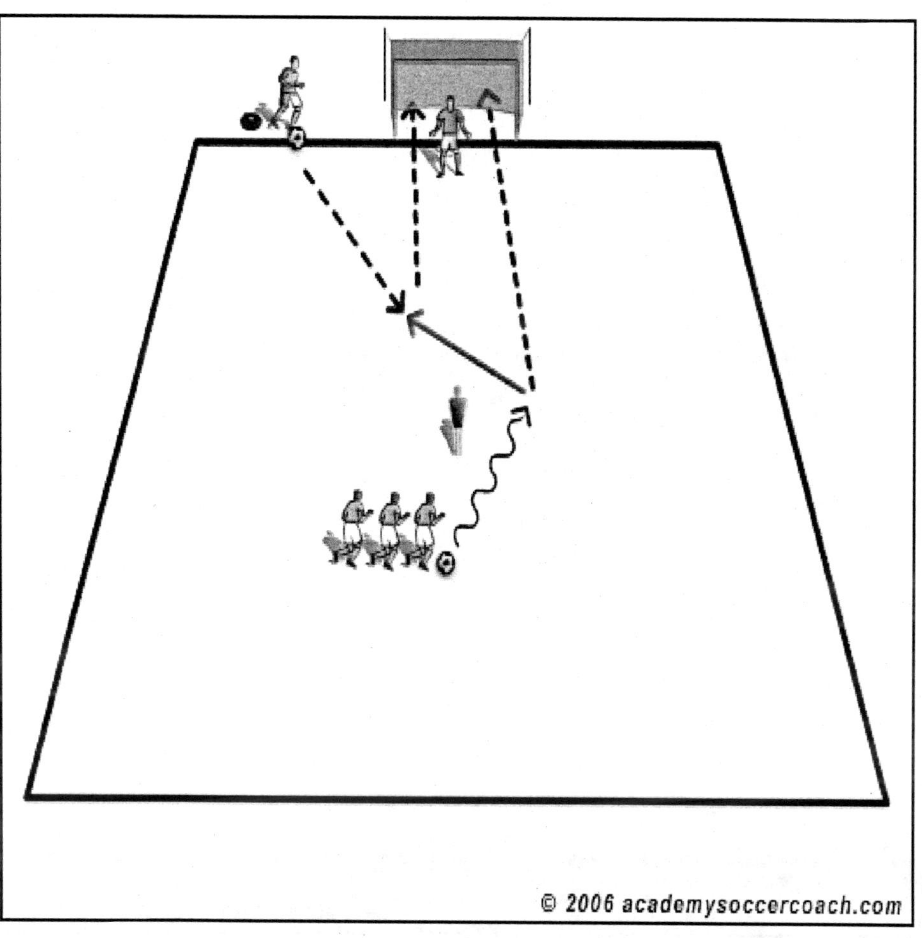

Practice 19

The attacker must dribble, complete a skill on the mannequin/cone and shoot with power
Immediately, the attacker must react and run to receive a pass from the coach
The attacker must now shoot from inside the box with a placed finish

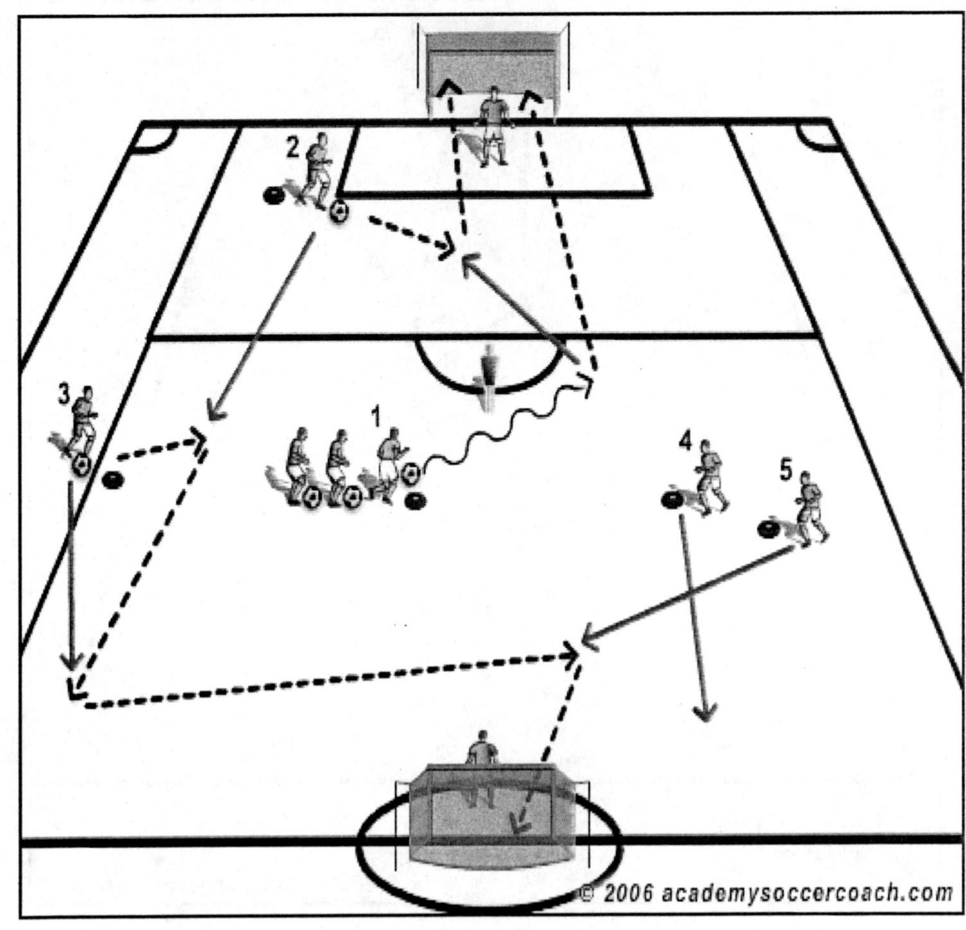

Practice 20

Player 1 must dribble , complete a skill on the mannequin/cone and shoot at goal
Immediately player 1 reacts and receives a pass from player 2
Player 1 now shoots for a 2nd time
Player 2 immediately reacts and runs to play a one-two with player 3
Player 3 now crosses for players 4 and 5
Players 4 and 5 must attempt to score from player 3's cross

After each attack, The players move to the next place on the circuit

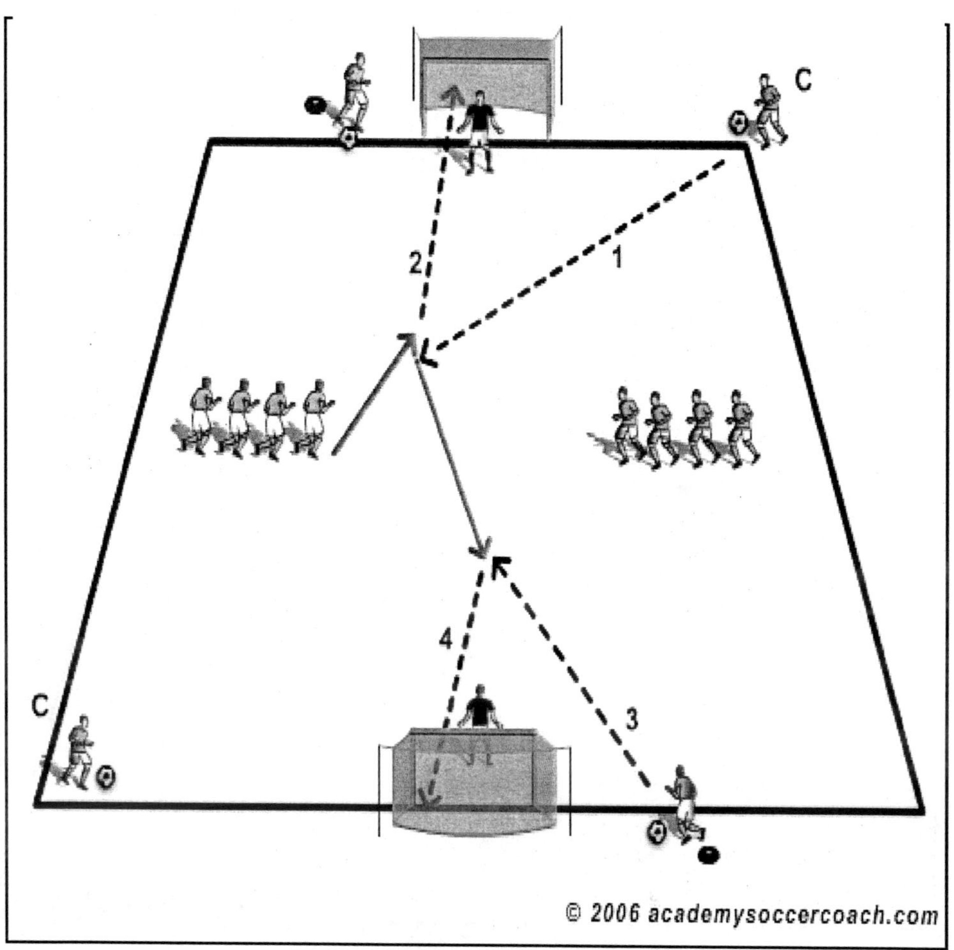

Practice 21

Two groups of players

Both groups work at the same time

To start, the coaches make diagonal passes (vary height, weight and type of pass)

The attackers must take one touch and then shoot at goal on their 2nd touch

Immediately the attackers must spin and run towards the opposite goal

Now the attacker receives a 2nd pass from a server and then shoots for a 2nd time

Rotation of players

After shooting, become the server and then join the opposite group

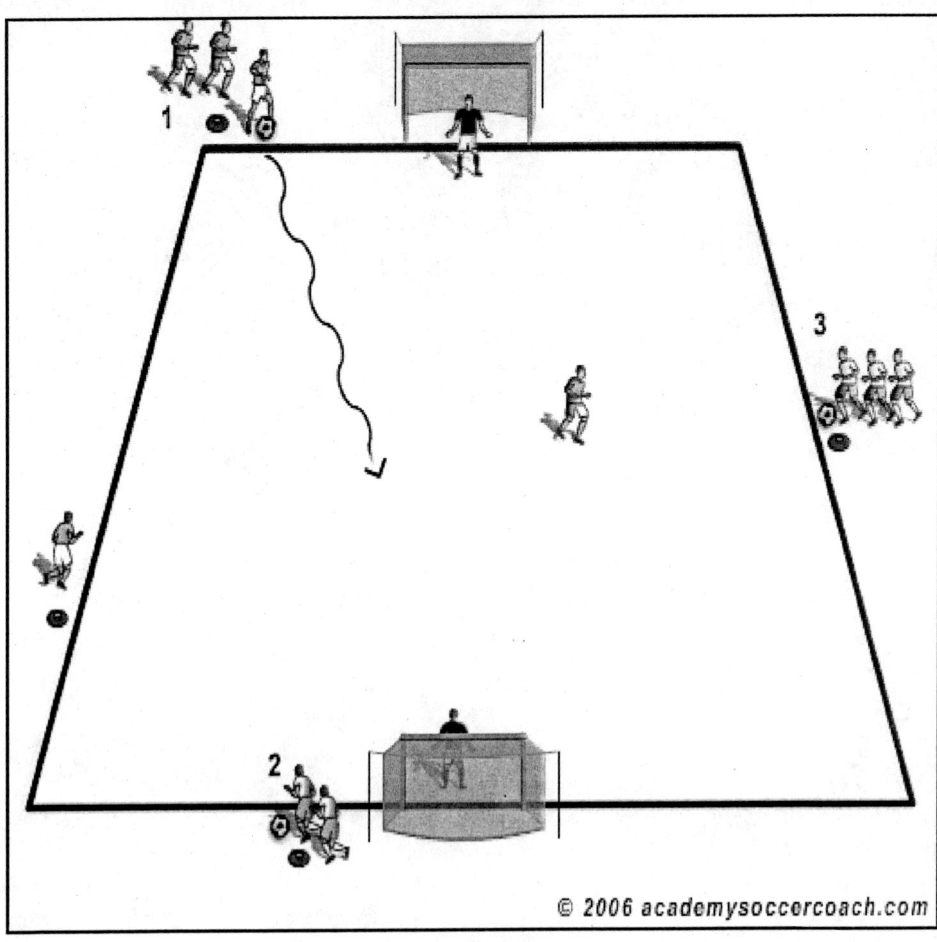

Practice 22

The practice has three stations

Station 1 – the attacker has three touches to dribble and score against the keeper
Station 2 – the defender passes to the attacker and then attempts to recover. The attacker must quickly dribble towards goal and attempt to score
Station 3 – the defender passes to the attacker and then attempts to stop him from scoring. The Attacker must show disguise and attempt to dribble and score in either of the goals

Rotation of players
After each turn, the players move to the next station.
On stations 2 and 3, the players are the defender 1st and then the attacker

Practice 23

This practice has three stations
The players work on the coaches whistle and must complete each role / position before moving to the next station

Station 1 – the attacker dribbles onto the pitch and a 1v1 game commences
Station 2 – the passer plays the ball into the attacker who must turn the defender and score
Station 3 – the defender passes into space, the attackers runs and attempts to score. Can the defender race back and stop him?

Roles / Positions
Station 1 – attacker then defender
Station 2 – passer, attacker and then defender
Station 3 – defender then attacker

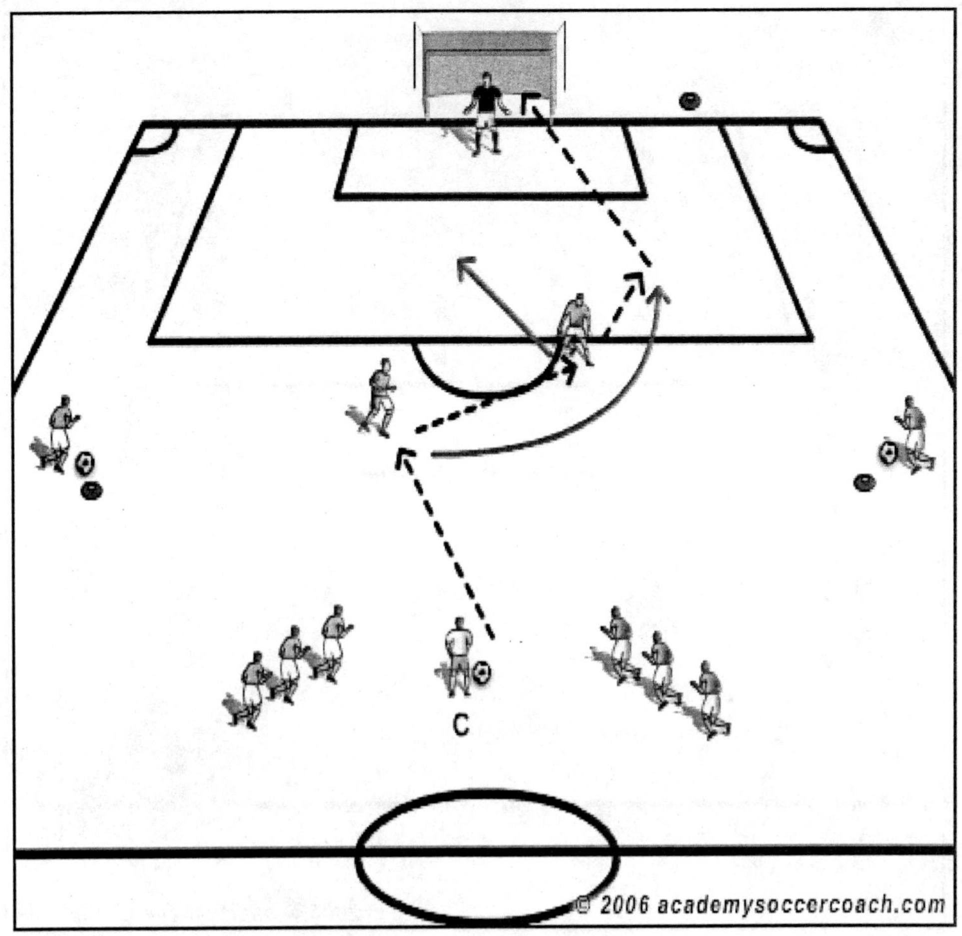

Practice 24

The coach passes into the two attackers
The two attackers must combine and then get a shot at goal

Now the attackers react and receive a 2nd ball from one of the wide servers
Again the two attackers must react and get a shot at goal

Finally, the attackers receive a 3rd ball from the last server and get a shot at goal

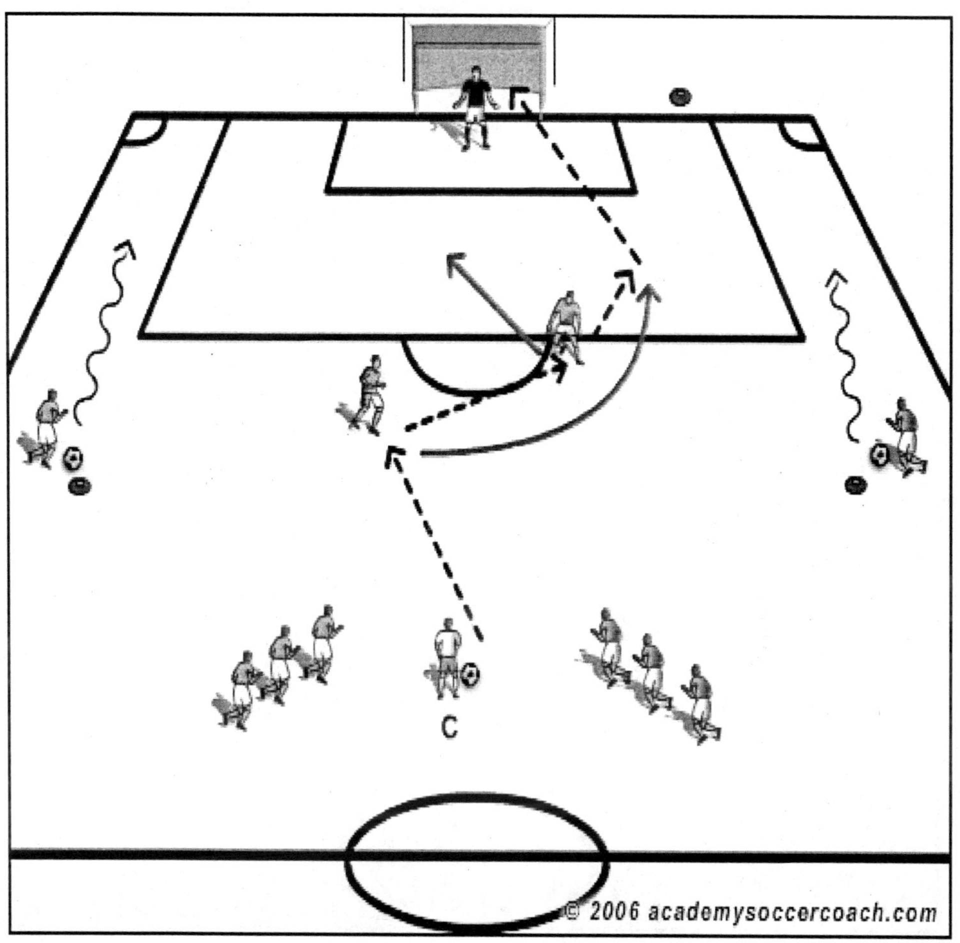

<u>Practice 25</u>

The two attackers receive a ball from the coach and combine to score
The attackers must now react to the coaches call of “left” or “right”

Immediately, the wide player called must either combine with the attackers and cross
Or dribble alone to the by-line and cross
The two attackers react and attempt to score

Finally, the attackers react to the other wide players cross and attempt to score for the 3rd time

Practice 26

Same as the previous drill but now the attackers are up against a defender

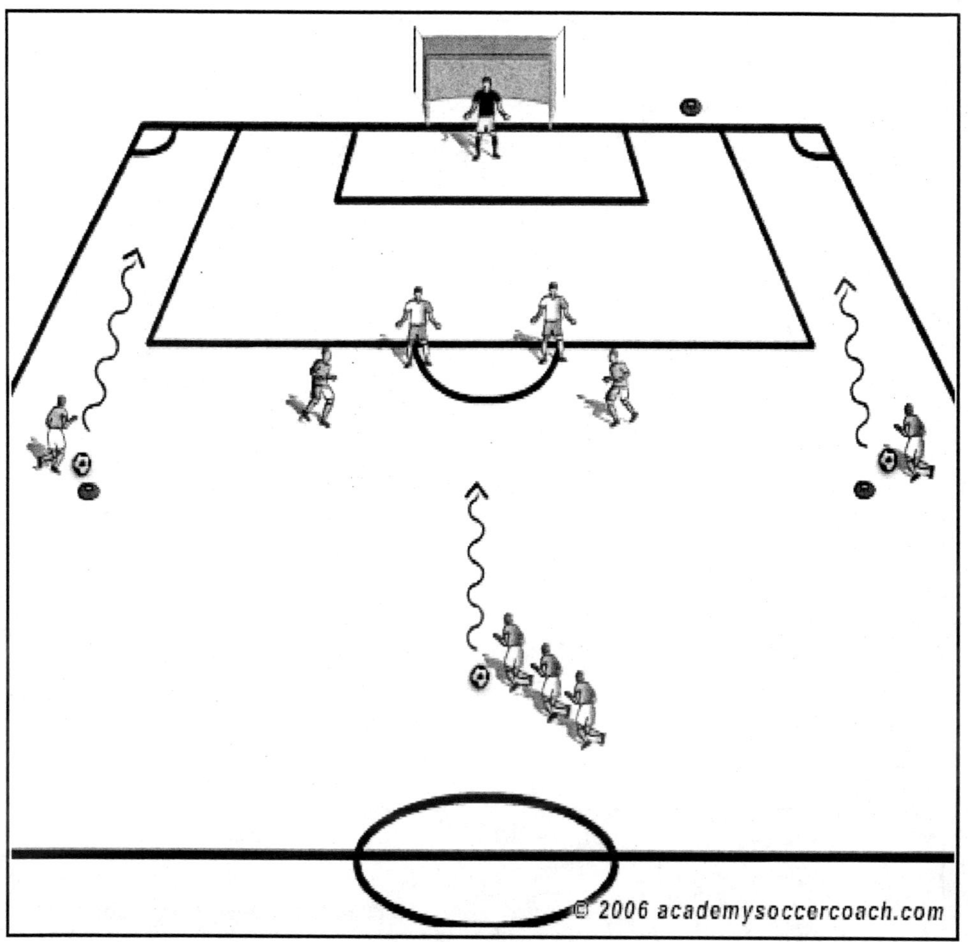

Practice 27

This time the drill contains two defenders
The starting player must dribble into the pitch to make a 3v2 situation with the attackers

The coach will then call out the wide player that combines with the three attackers and get a cross into the box

Can the three attackers lose the two defenders and score?

Finally, the attackers eact for a 3rd time and look to score from the other wide players cross

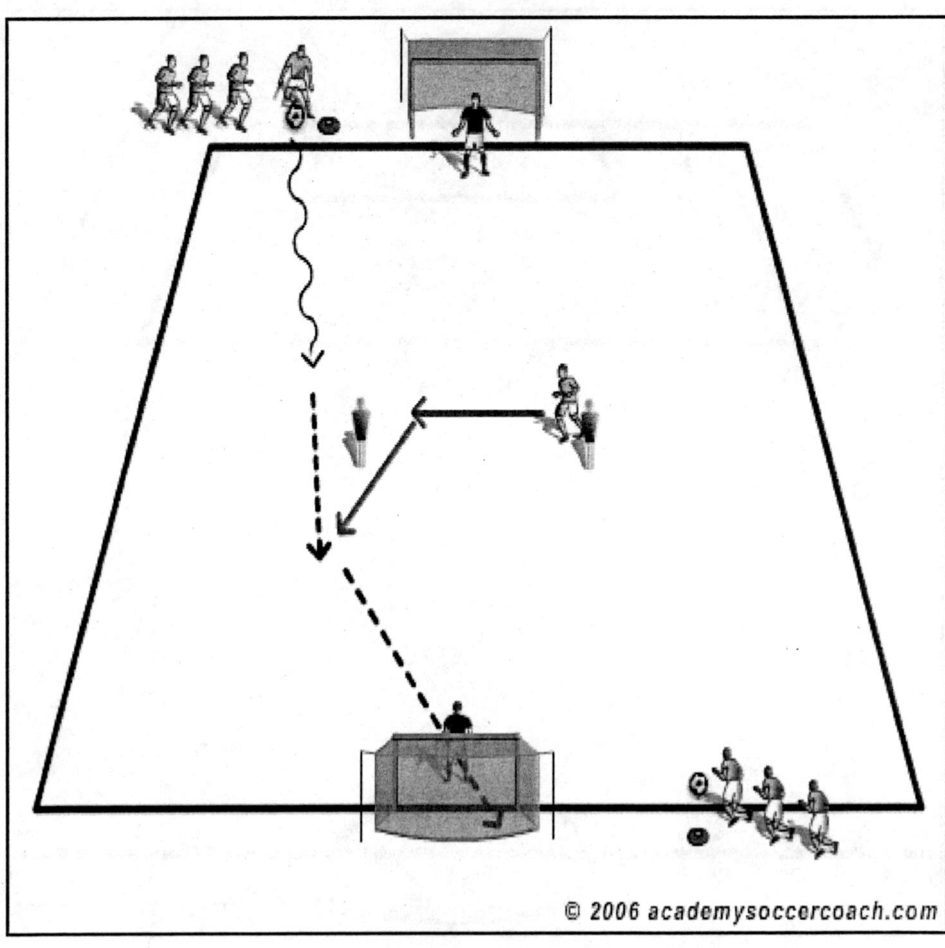

Practice 28

Two groups of players
The dribbling players run with the ball at full pace towards the mannequin
The forward makes a run along the line of the mannequins and then into the space behind
the dribbling player makes a through pass for the forward
The forward attempts to score with a first time shot

Immediately, the attack comes from the opposite end
The original dribbling player is now a forward and must react quickly to make his run and score

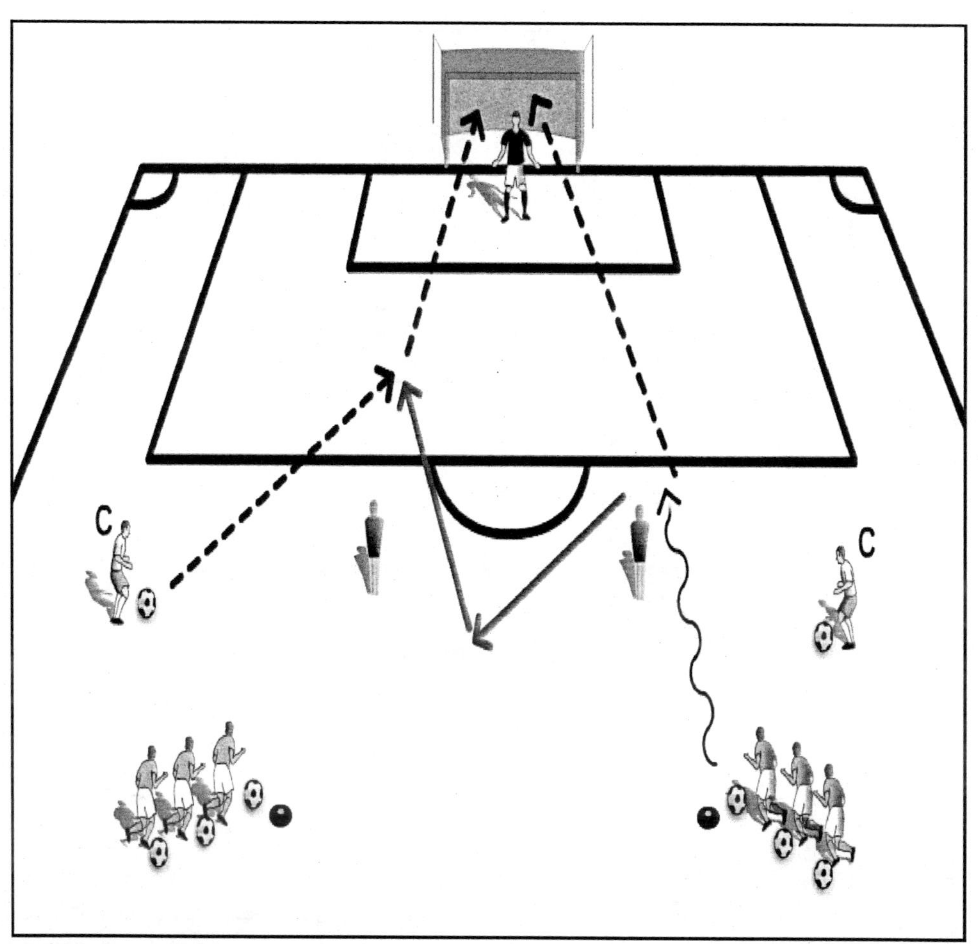

Practice 29

The attackers must dribble, complete a skill and then shoot at goal

Then the attacker must react and quickly get back onside

Once back onside, the attacker makes another run in behind the mannequin

Once a 2nd ball is played into space by the coach.

The forward races after the ball and gets a 2nd shot at goal

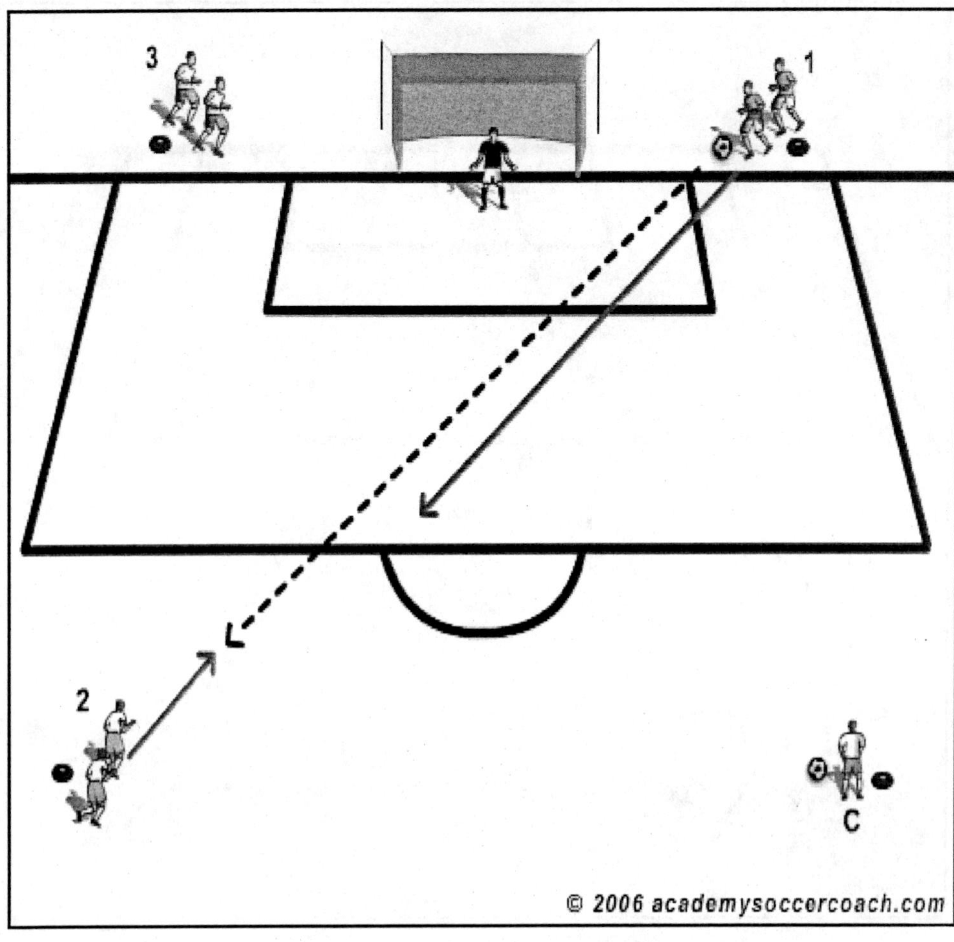

Practice 30

Player 1 passes to player 2
Player 2 now attempts to take on player 1 and score against the keeper

Once this ball is played, the coach passes a 2nd ball into player 1
Immediately player 3 runs out and attempts to stop player 1 from turning and shooting at goal

For the next attack, player 1 becomes player 2 and player 2 becomes player 3
And player 3 becomes player 1

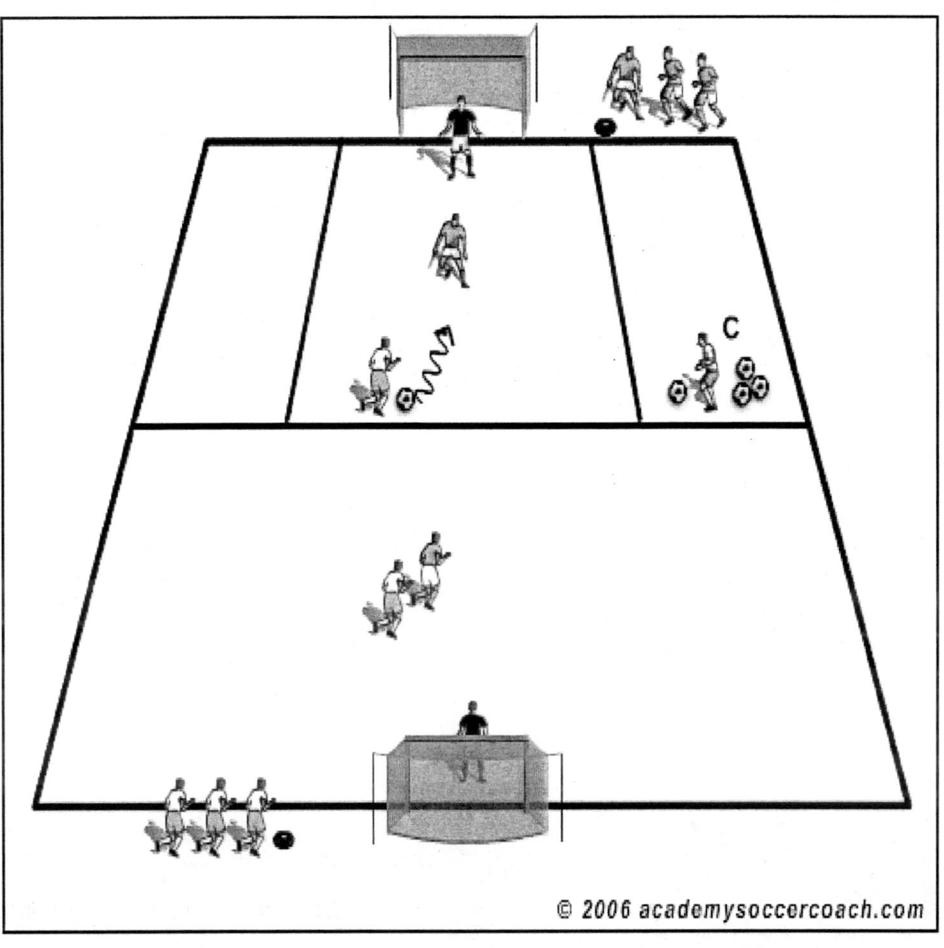

<u>Practice 31</u>

One team attacks 1v1 and then defends 1v2
The other team defends 1v1 and then attacks 2v1
After each attack, the coach passes a new ball to the attacking team

The game is played for a set time period with the coach keeping scores the team switch roles for the next game.

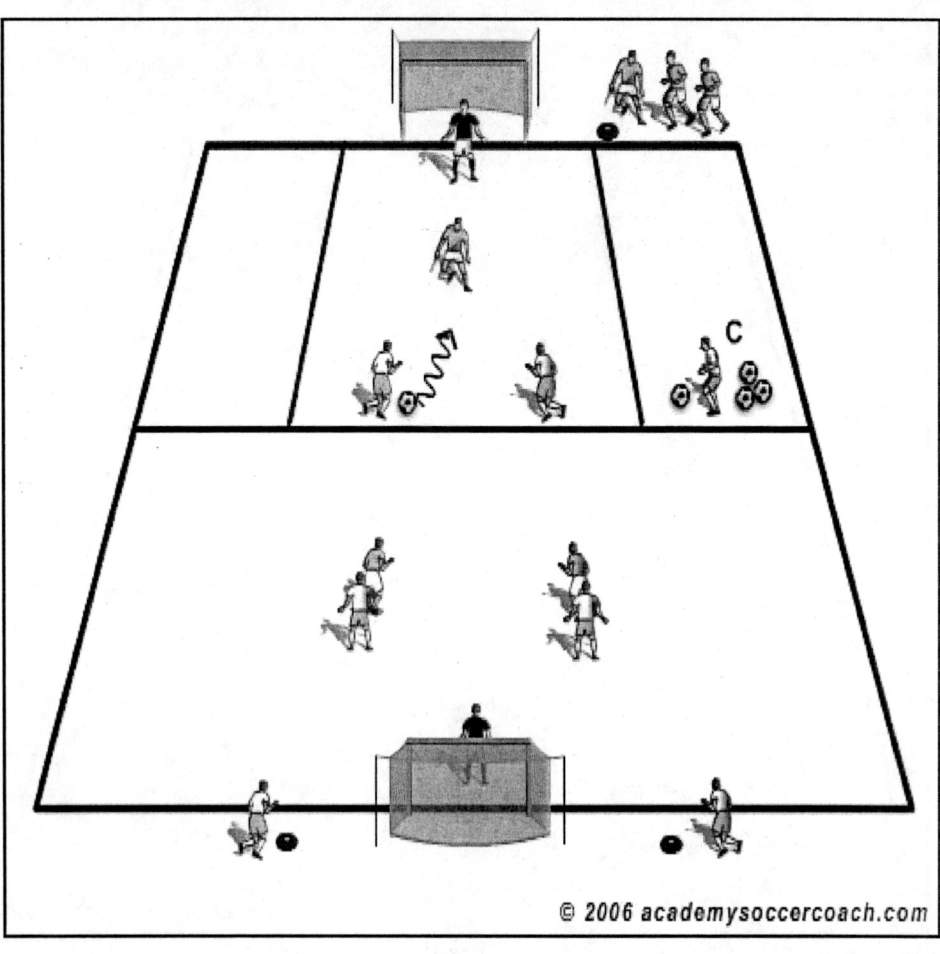

<u>Practice 32</u>

One team attacks 2v1 and then defends 2v3
The other team defends 1v2 and then attacks 3v2
After each attack, the coach passes a new ball to the attacking team

The game is played for a set time period with the coach keeping scores
the team switch roles for the next game.

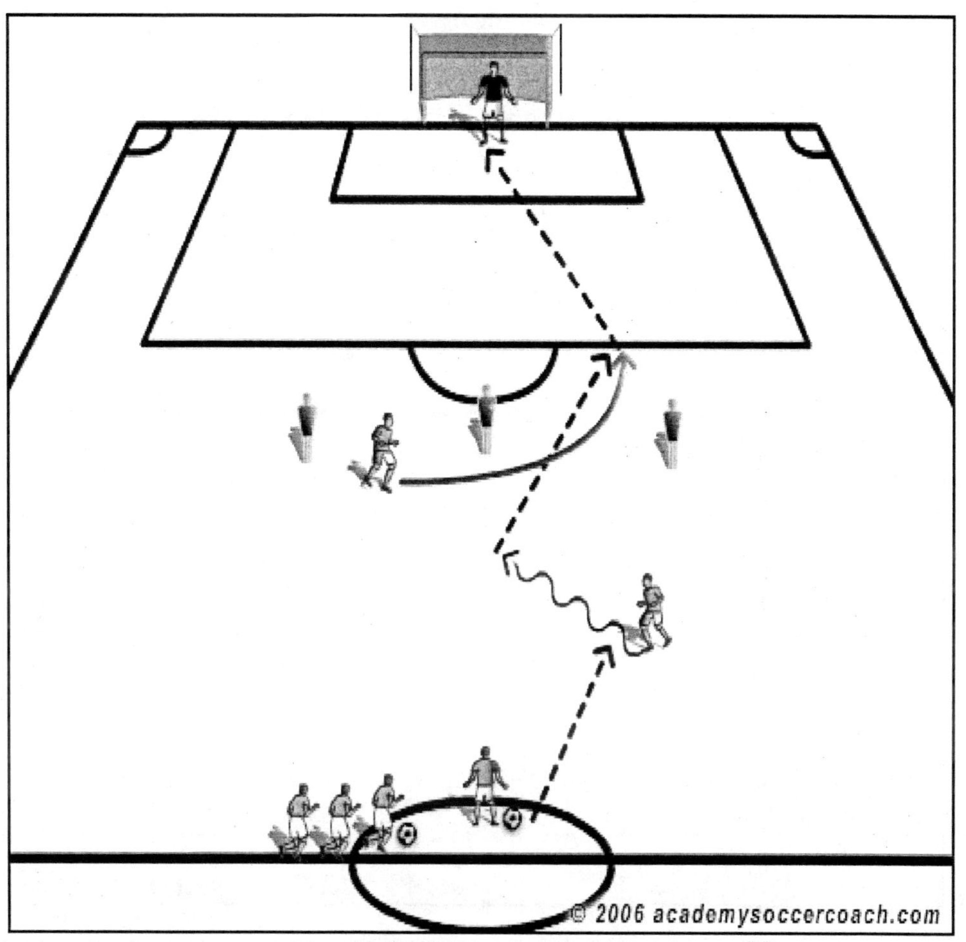

<u>Practice 33</u>

The midfielder must make an angled movement in order to receive a pass
the midfielder must receive the ball side on and then dribble towards the mannequin
The midfielder must look up whilst dribbling and make a through pass for the forward
The forward receives the pass in space and then shoots at goal

The forward is allowed complete freedom of movement.
The coach should encourage the forwards to use their imagination.

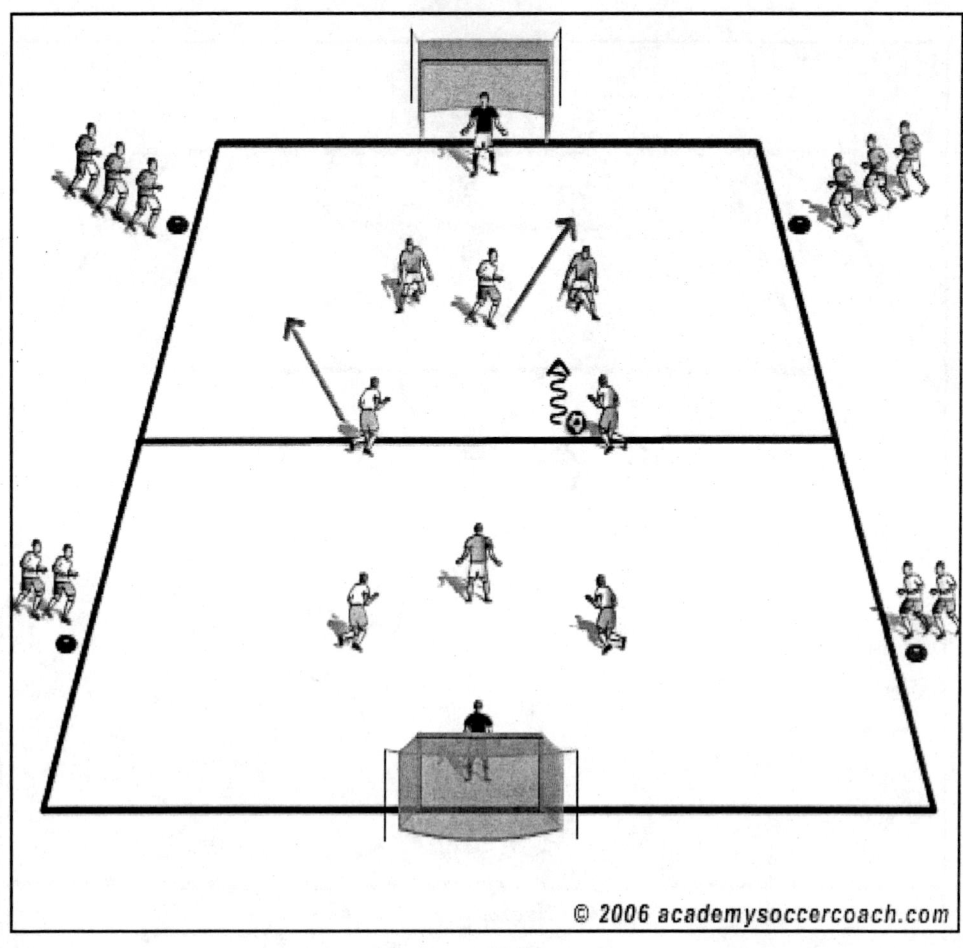

<u>Practice 34</u>

Two teams

Each team selects a forward that is always on the pitch

the remaining players are divided into pairs

The starting team attack in a 3v2 situation

Once this attack is completed, the two opposite defenders make a counter attack to the opposite goal

Now this team have a 3v2 situation

Each time the defenders break out to counter attack, two new players must take up their positions

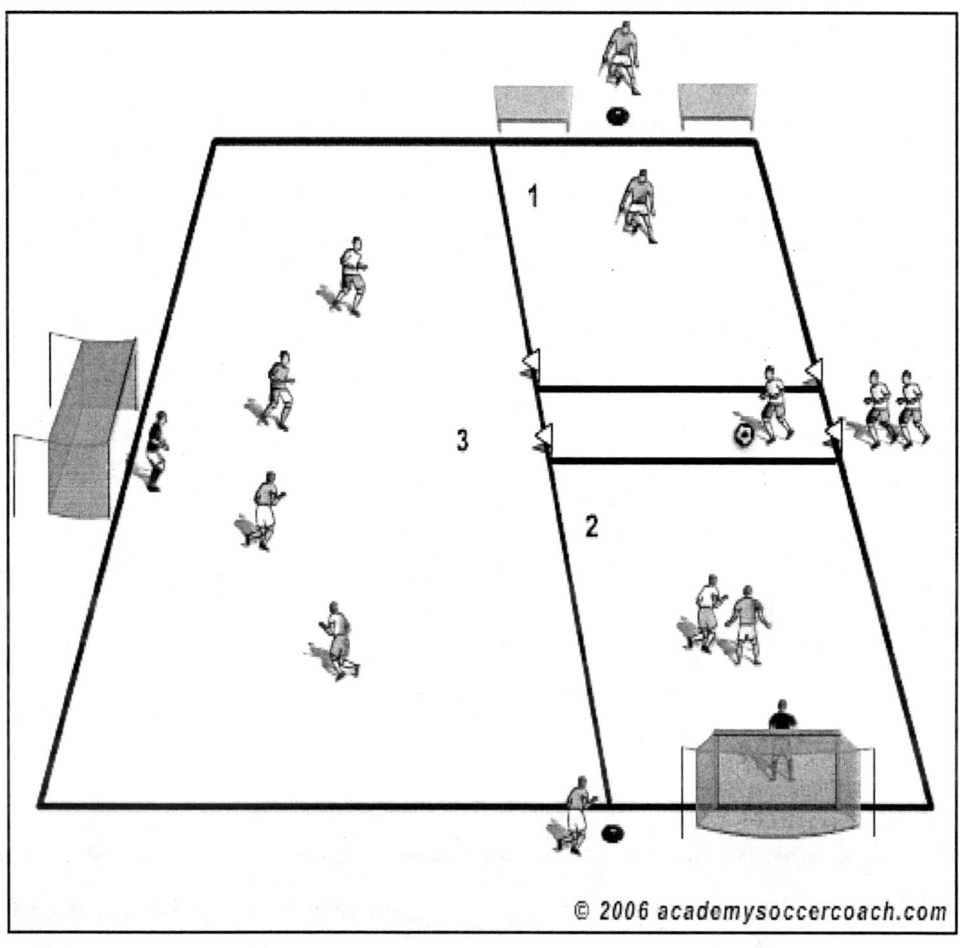

Practice 35

Two teams of six players
One team work as the attackers
The other team work as defenders
After a set time, the roles are reversed

The defending team must have two players on each pitch as shown above

Pitch 1 – 1v1 situation into two target goals
Pitch 2 – 2v1 overload
Pitch 3 – 3v2 situation

The attacker in possession of the ball has a choice of which pitch to attack.
The only rule is that you must attack a different pitch on each turn

*after attacking onto pitch 2 or 3. you must stay on the pitch and let a different attacker come out.
This enables all attackers to have the choice of dribbling into the pitch of their choice.

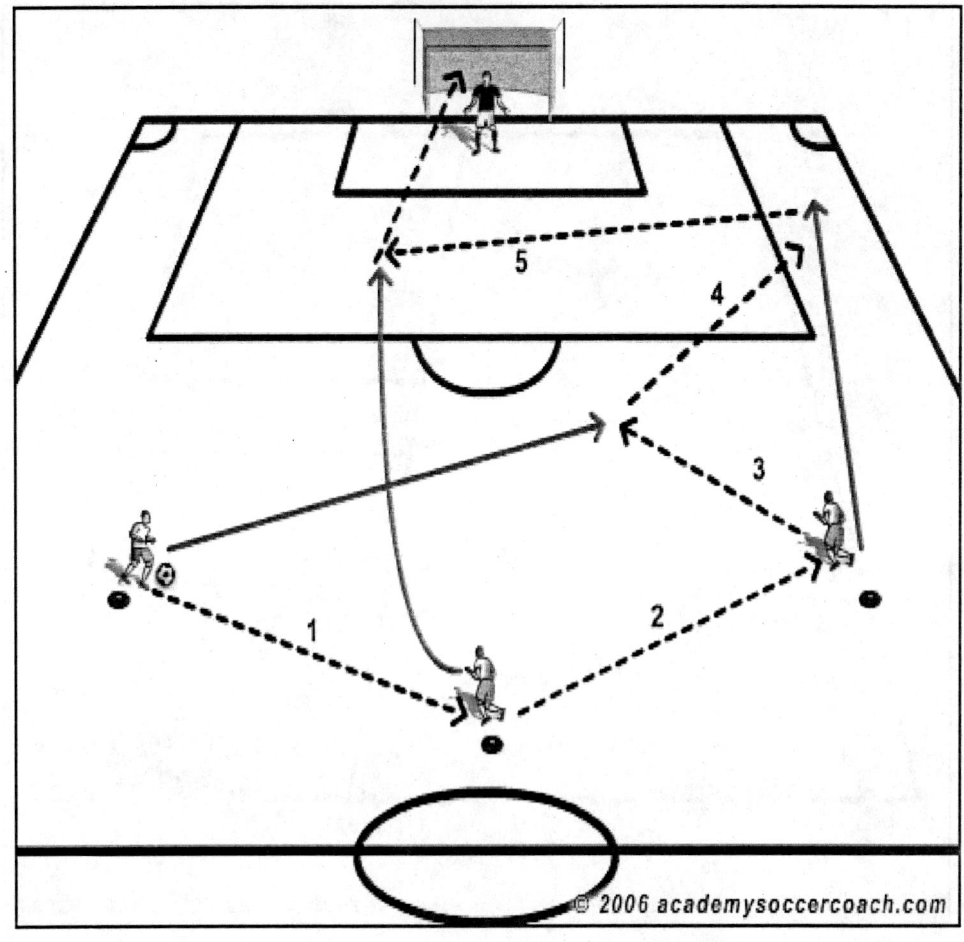

Practice 36

This practice includes lots of fluent passing and movements off the ball

To start, the ball is transferred from the left midfielder to the centre midfielder
The left midfielder now makes a diagonal run into the centre of the pitch

The centre midfielder receives the pass and then opens out to pass to the right midfielder.
The right midfielder plays into the left midfielder and runs down the line to receive a return pass

The centre midfielder makes a run into the box and attempts to score first time.
If he is unable to score first time then he must set the left midfielder who has made a supporting run

For the next attack, the left midfielder becomes the centre midfielder
The centre midfielder becomes the right midfielder
The right midfielder rests and waits to become the new left midfielder

Practice 37

To start, the first player dribbles and passes to the central player
The central player then passes out to a wide player and makes an overlapping run
The wide player now dribbles inside and then makes a reverse pass to the overlapping player
The overlapping player crosses the ball into the wide player
The wide player attempts to score

For the next attack, the first player becomes the new central player
The central player takes the place of the wide player
The wide player rest and waits for their next turn

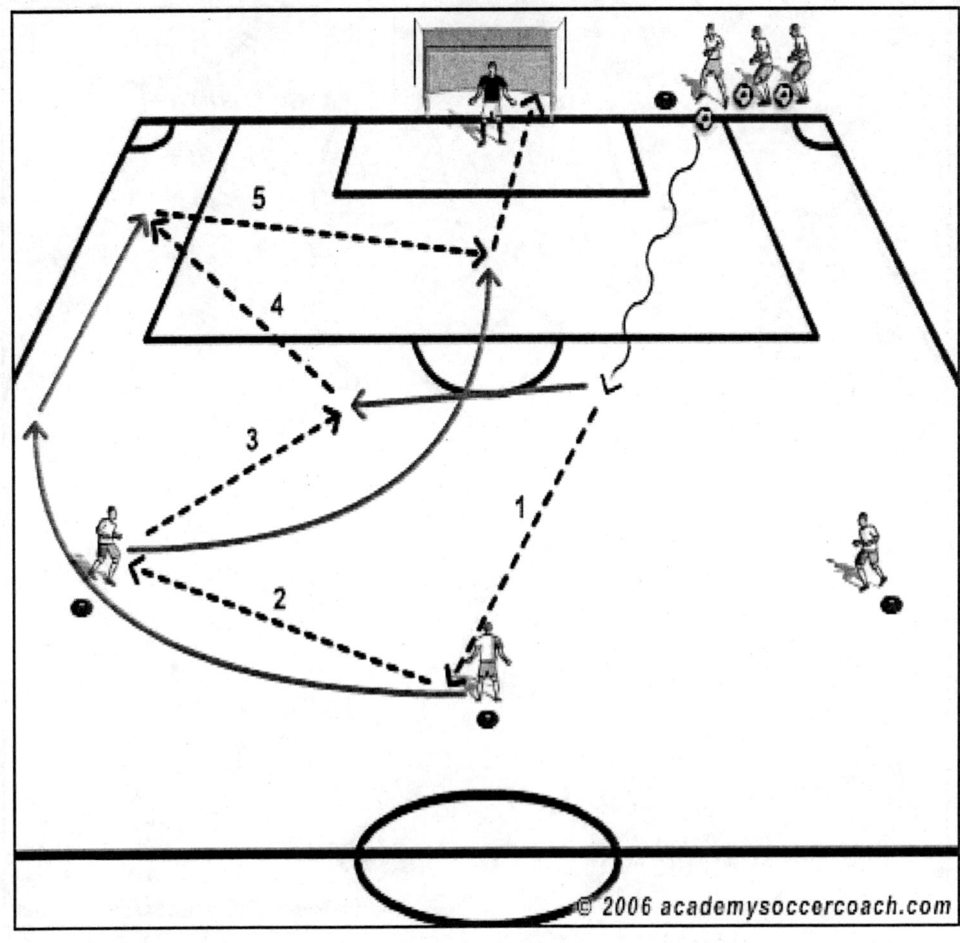

Practice 38

This practice is a progression to the practice 37

The only change is that the first player now plays a 2nd role in the attack.
After passing to the central player, the first player must now get ready to play a wall pass.

When the wide player receives the ball he now plays into the first player and then gets into the box
The first player passes first time into space for the overlapping player to run and cross.

The rotation of players is the same as in practice 37

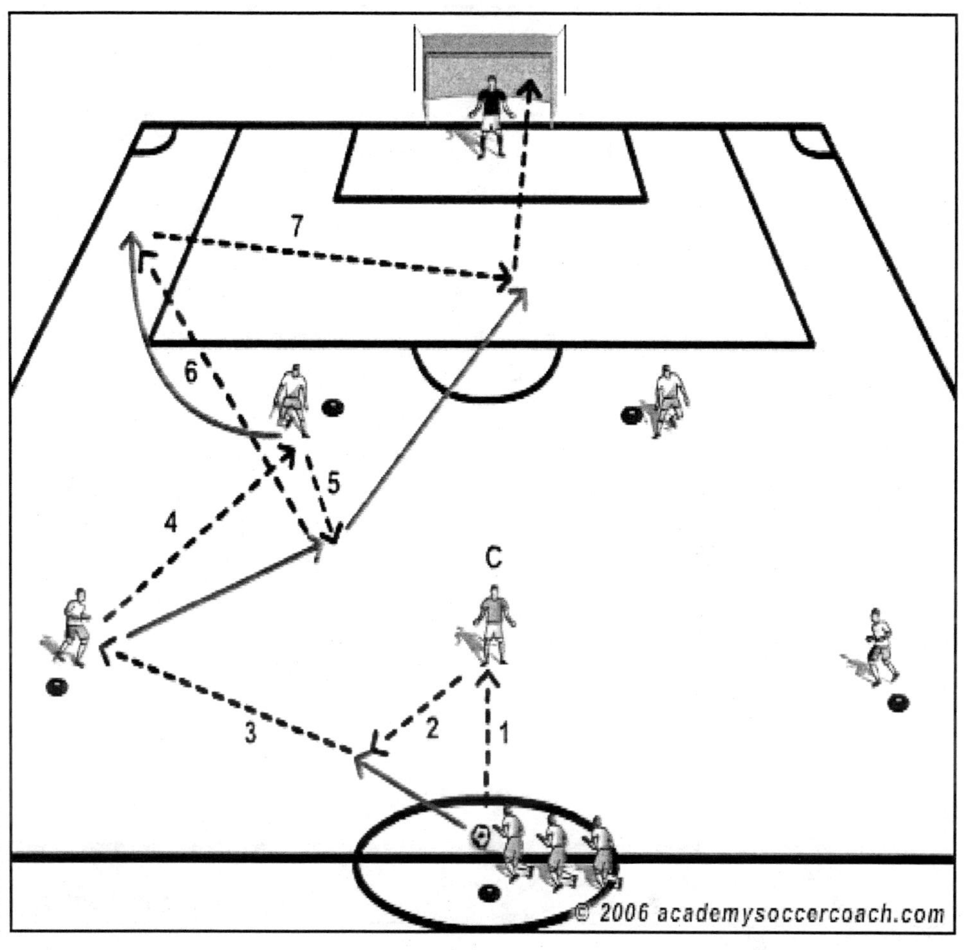

<u>Practice 39</u>

The starting player makes a one-two with the coach and then passes to the wide player
The wide player then passes into the forward and makes a run inside
The forward passes back to the wide player and then spins outside
The wide player returns the pass to the forward and then gets into the box
The forward crosses for the wide player who must attempt to score

For the next attack, the starting player becomes a wide player
The wide player becomes a forward
The forward returns to the beginning and waits to become a starting player

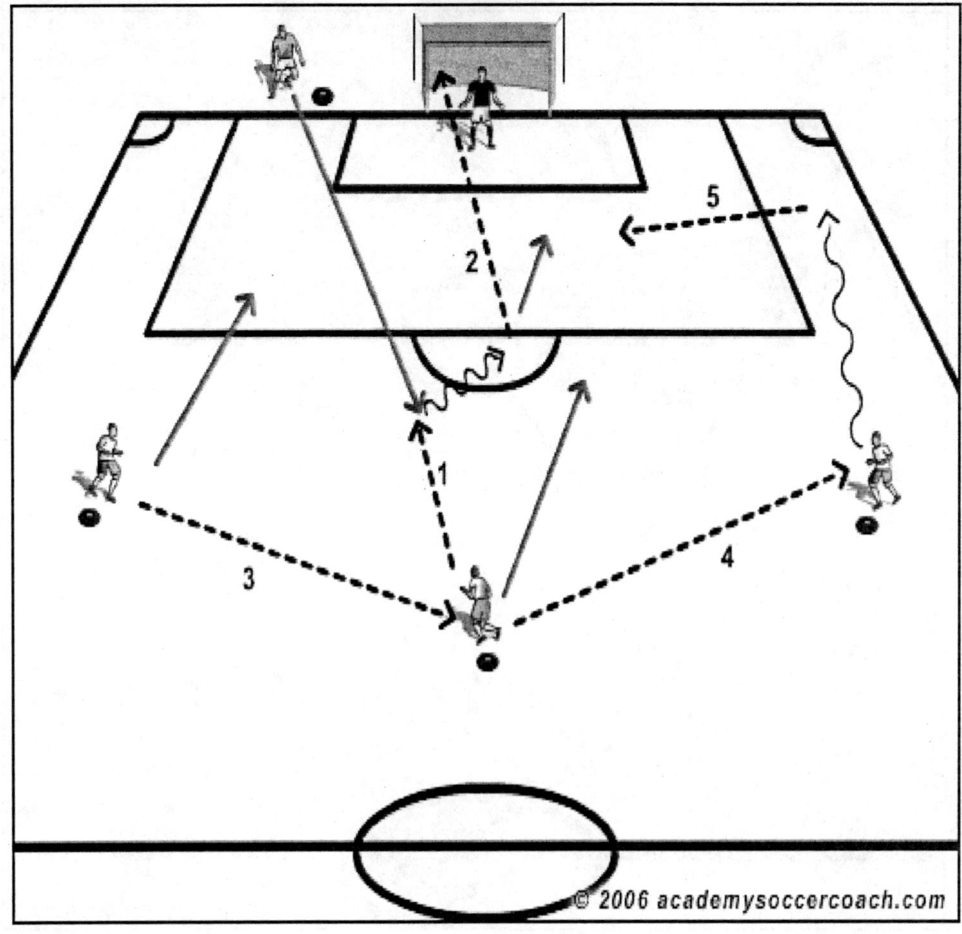

Practice 40

To start, the defender runs out and receives a pass from the middle player
The defender must quickly turn and shoot at goal

As soon as the defender has taken a touch of the ball, the left player passes into the middle player
The middle player now switches the ball out to the right player
The right player dribbles down the line and crosses into the box
Can the left and middle players lose the defender and score?

For the next attack
The left player becomes the middle player
The middle player becomes the right player
The right player becomes the defender
The defender becomes the left player

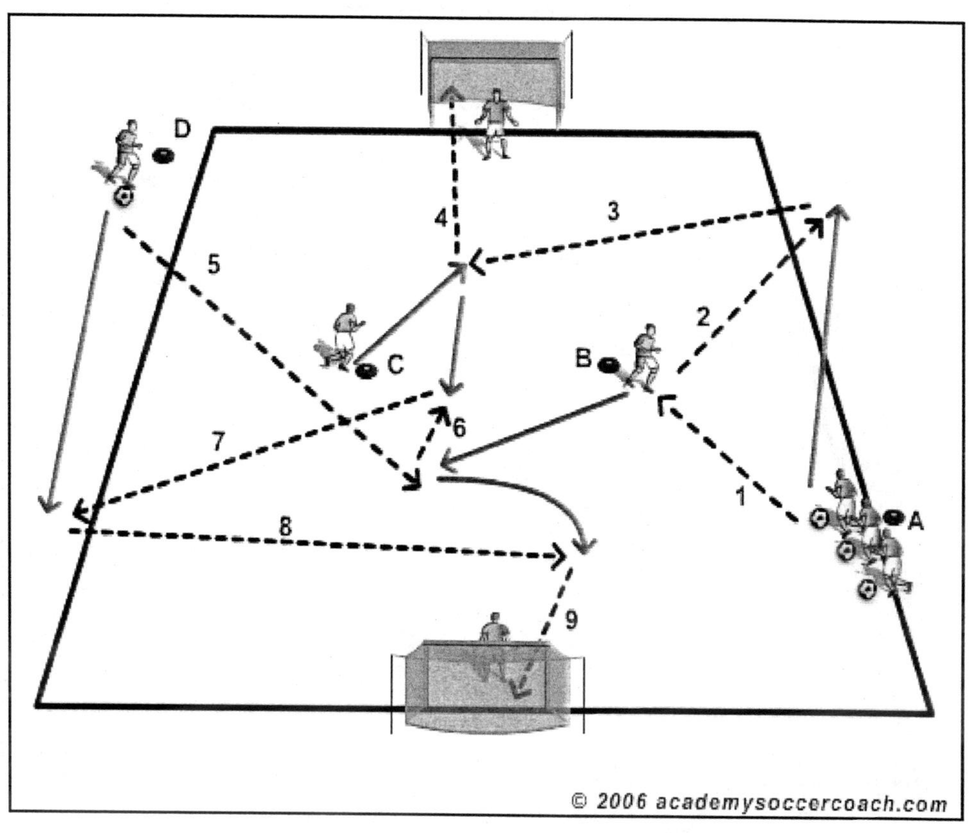

Practice 41

Both forwards will receive crosses to score
The practice has four playing positions A,B,C,D
After playing in one position you must move to the next position

To start, player A plays a one-two with player B and crosses for C
After playing the one-two, player B moves diagonally towards the opposite goal

Now, player D passes long into player B,
Player B lays the ball back to player C who has reacted after scoring from the original cross
Player C no plays the ball down the line for player D
Player D crosses for player B to score

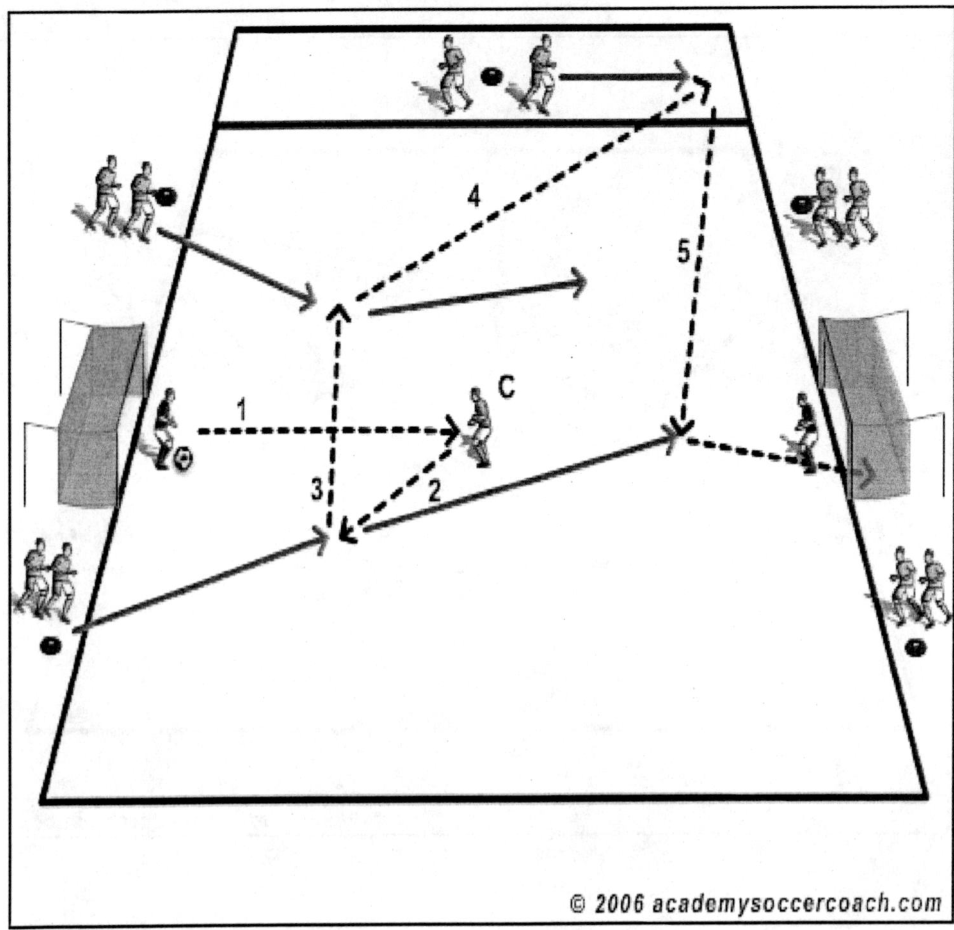

Practice 42

The keeper starts the practice by throwing the ball into the coach
Two attackers make supporting runs in order to receive the coaches lay off
The two attackers must quickly combine and then pass out to the wide player
The wide player then crosses for the two attackers to score

Immediately the opposite keeper throws the ball into the coach
The practice now works in the opposite direction

Practice 43

replace the coach with a defender
The defender must set the ball and then react and try to defend the cross

Practice 44

Add two defenders and a forward. The two defenders must allow the forward to set the ball
The defenders are only allowed to defend on the cross
Can the three forwards make movements to score off the cross?

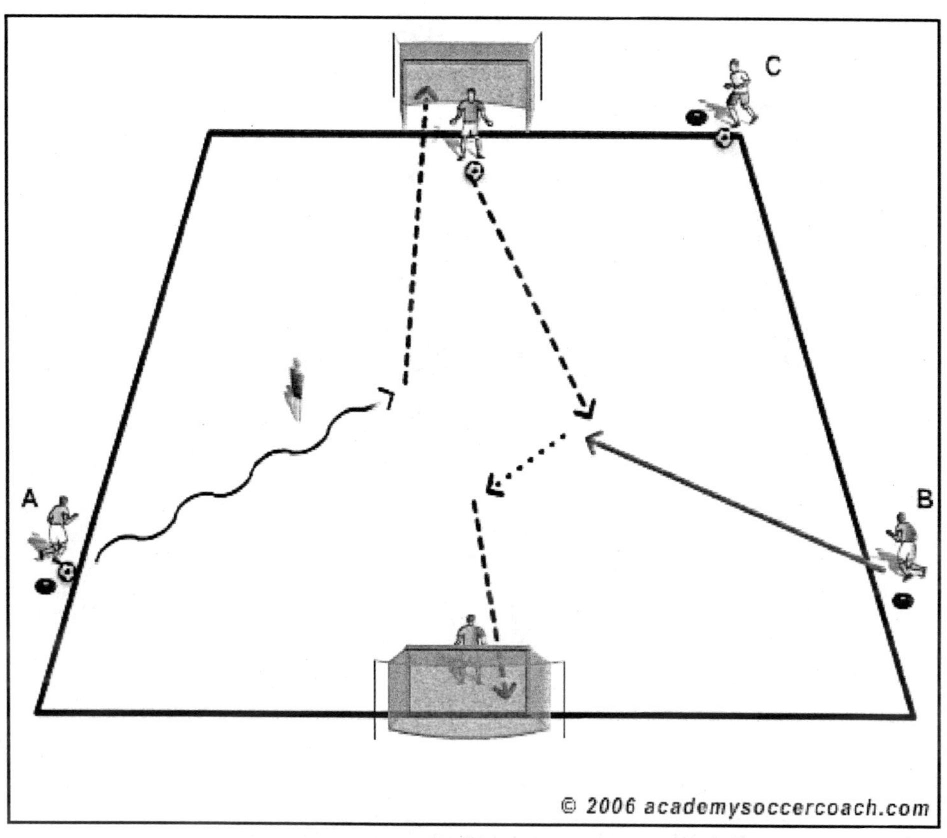

Practice 45

Players A and B work at the same time
Player A dribbles and goes past the mannequin to shoot
Player B receives a throw from the keeper and turns to shoot at the opposite goal
Now player C comes into the practice by passing into players A and B
The two players must combine with each other and then pass wide for player C
Player C now crosses for players A and B to score

Progression
Give player C the choice of going wide or making a run onto the pitch for a 3rd man run
The forwards must now combine and make a through pass for player C to score

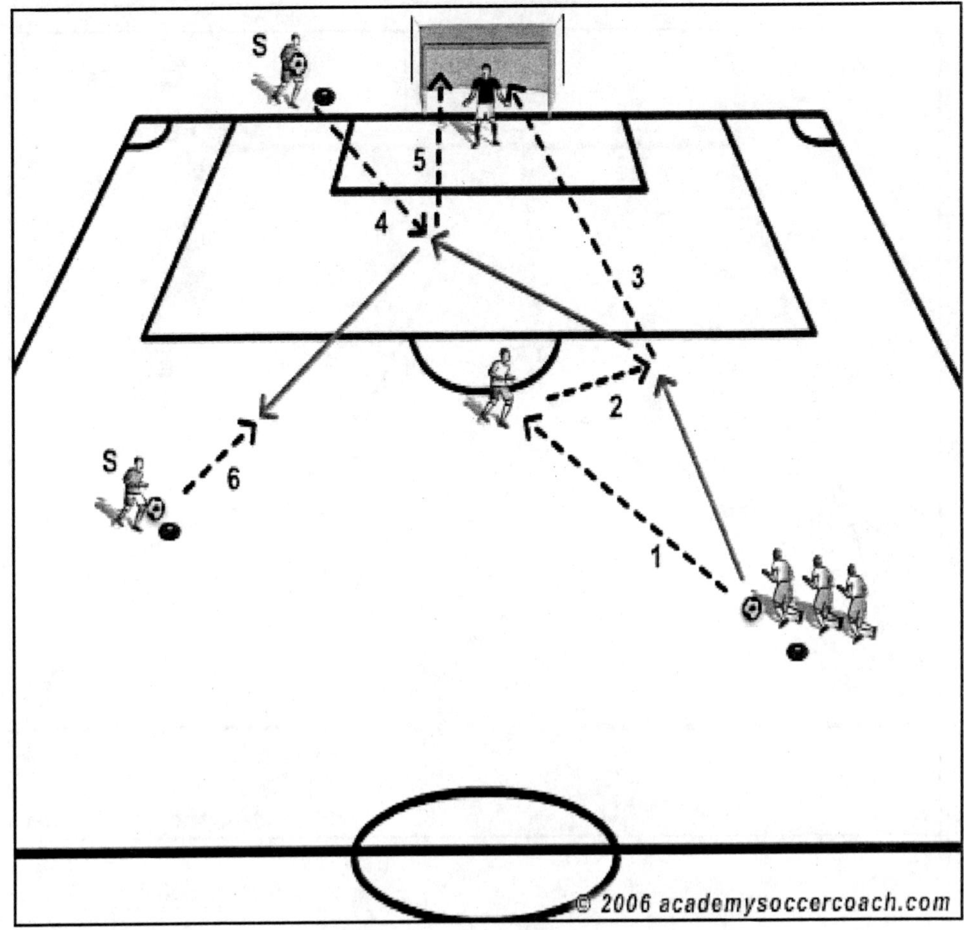

Practice 46

The shooting player must complete three exercises

1 – pass into the target player and run to receive a return pass and shoot
2 – now react and run to the server in order to receive an aerial pass to head at goal
3 – now run to the last server and receive a pass to turn and shoot at goal

The shooting player must now become the target player

"Who can score a hat-trick?"

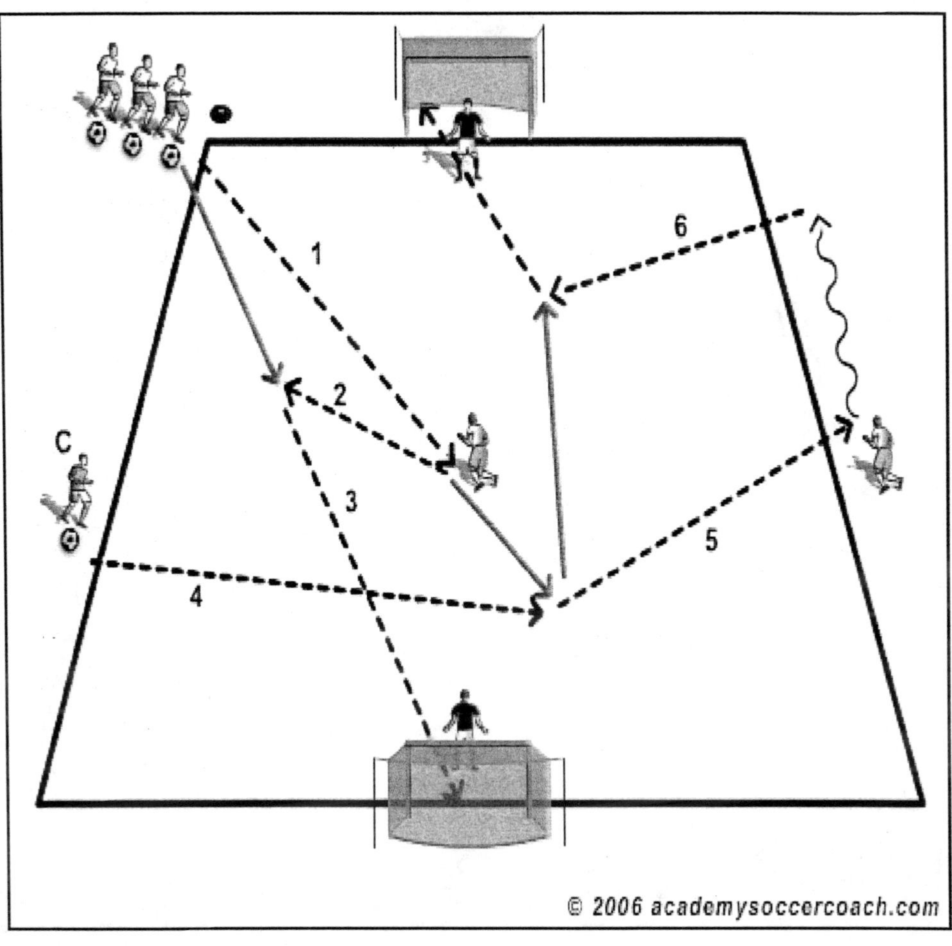

Practice 47

The starting player passes into the forward and makes a supporting run.
The forward sets the starting player up for a shot at goal
The forward must react and look for any rebounds

Immediately after this ball has been played. The forward receives a 2nd pass from the coach
The forward must now switch the play out to the crosser
The forward makes a run towards the opposite goal and attempts to score on the cross

For the next attack
The starting player becomes the forward
The forward becomes the crosser
The crosser joins the back of the line and waits to become a starting player

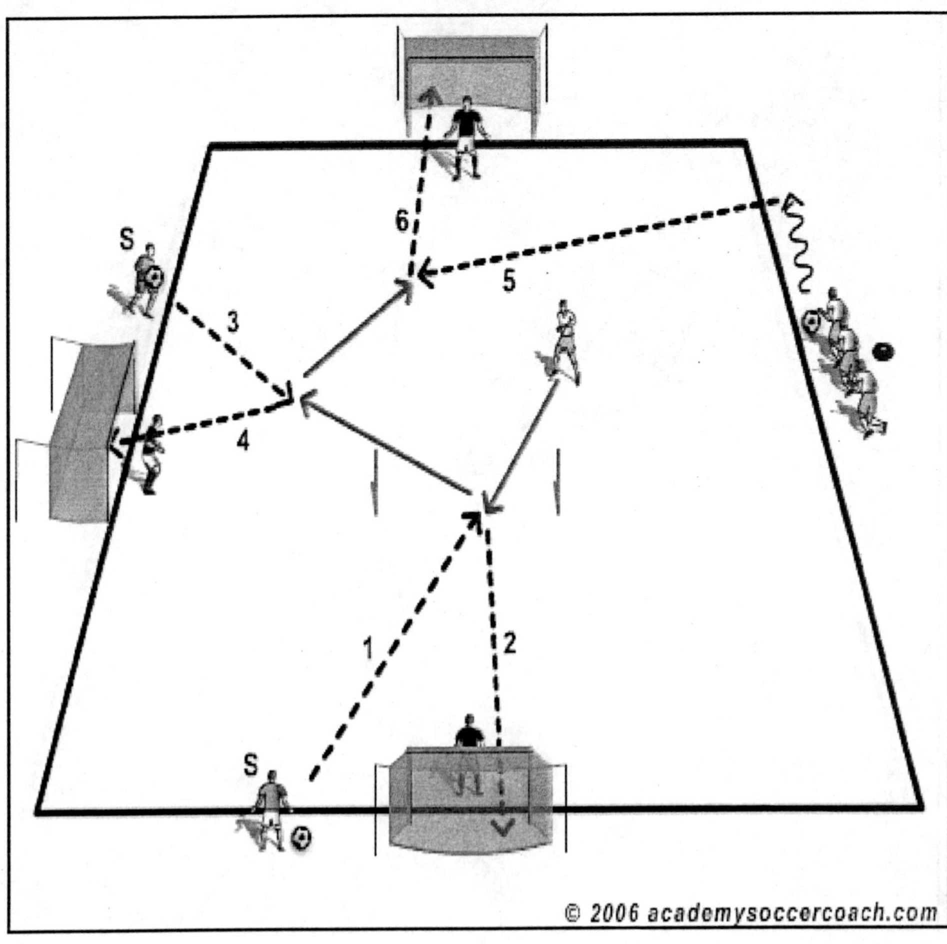

Practice 48

The working player has two complete three finishing exercises

To start, the player has to run through the gate and receive a pass in order to shoot 1st time
The player then reacts and runs back through the gate in order to receive an aerial serve
in order to head at goal. Finally, the player reacts again and gets into the box to receive a cross

The crossing player then becomes the new working player.

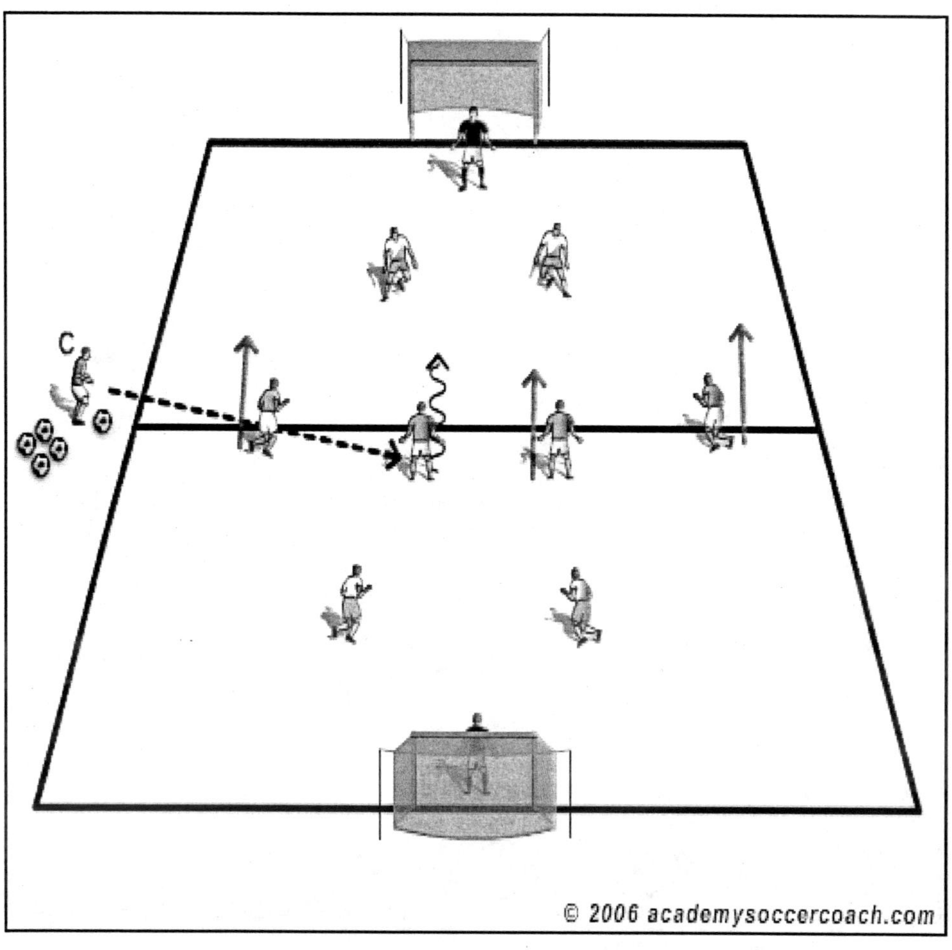

Practice 49

Two teams of four players
Two goalkeepers

The attacking team start on the middle line
The defending team split into pairs and go into separate halves of the pitch

To start, the coach passes to the attacking team
The attacking team have 10 continuous attacks (five at each goal)

After each ball has been played, the coach passes the team a new ball and they attack the opposite goal

Which team scores the most goals in their 10 attacks?

By reducing the number of touches allowed by each player, do you increase the number of goals?

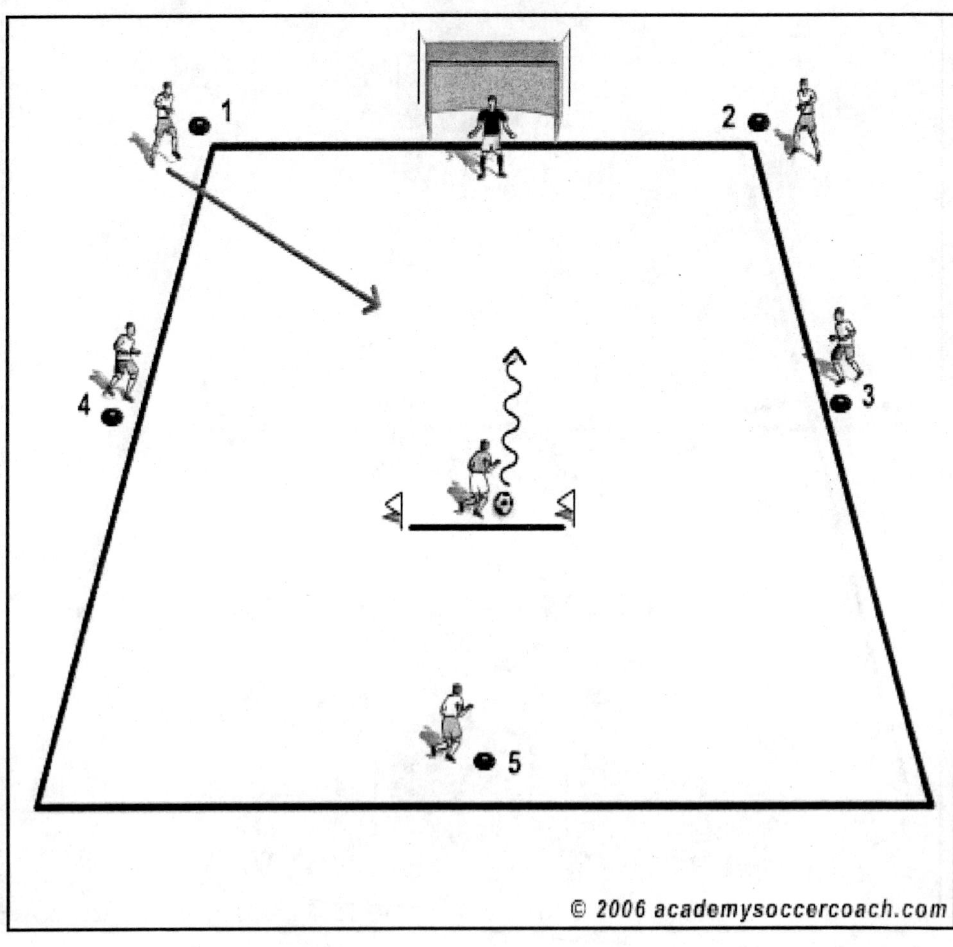

Practice 50

The attacking player starts with the ball and waits for the coaches call to attack
The five defenders are given a number

The coach calls out the number of the player to defend
The defender sprints and attempts to stop the attacker from scoring

The attacker and defender switch roles for the next turn.

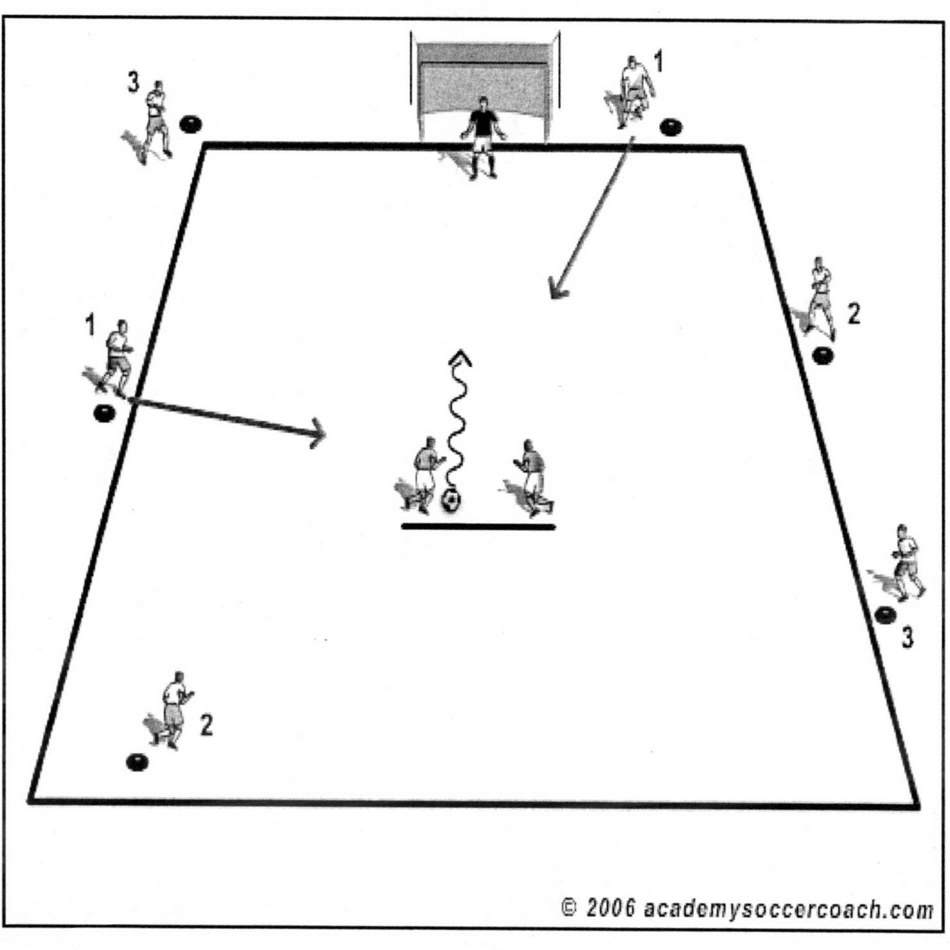

Practice 51

This practice is a progression of practice 50

The only difference is that the game is now 2v2 with defenders again coming from various angles

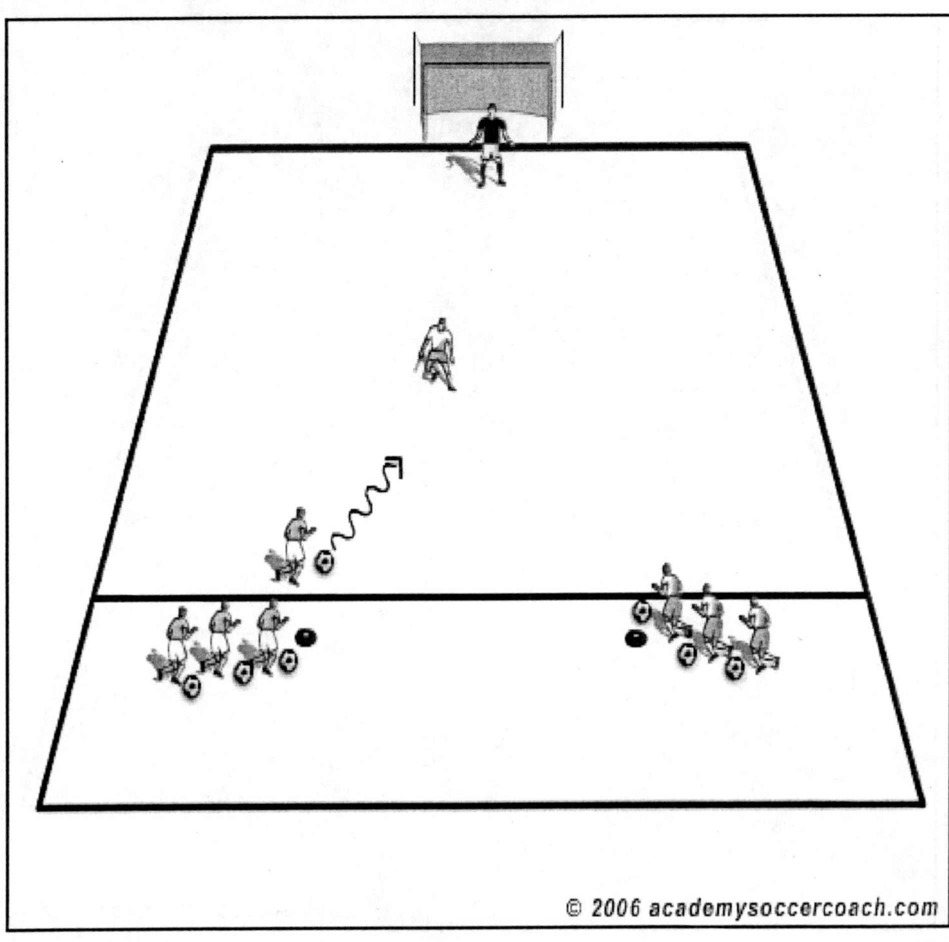

Practice 52

Two teams of players
One goalkeeper

The two teams take it in turns to attack 1v1 and then react to defend 1v1
The game is played until a certain number of goals are scored.

The player must continually react to the next ball
Encourage the attackers to be direct in their play and look to shoot at every opportunity

Practice 53

A progression on the above.
If the attacker scores a goal, then he does not have to defend and his team keep attacking until They stop scoring. E.g. – one team can score five continuous goals and win the game. this puts pressure on the defenders to defend to their maximum and stop the attackers from scoring

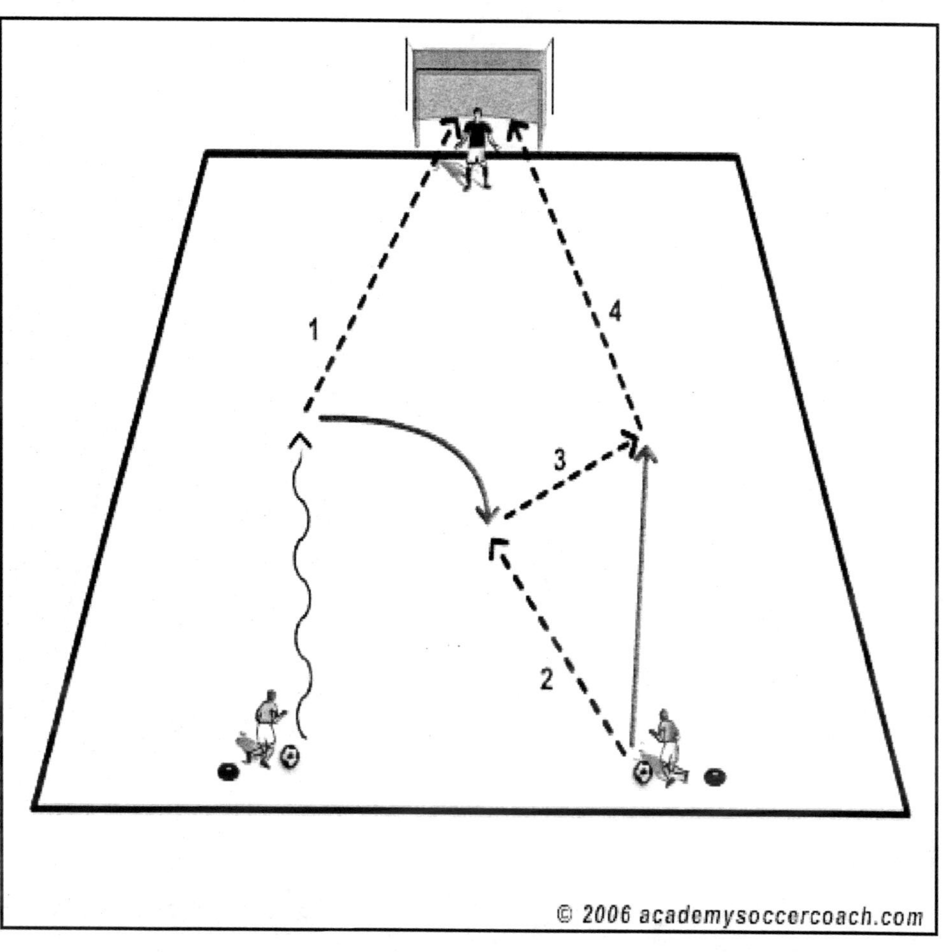

Practice 54

Player 1 dribbles and shoots at goal
Immediately player 1 spins and plays a wall pass for player 2 to shoot at goal
Player 1 follows the shot in order to get any rebounds off the keeper or posts.

The players switch roles for the next attack

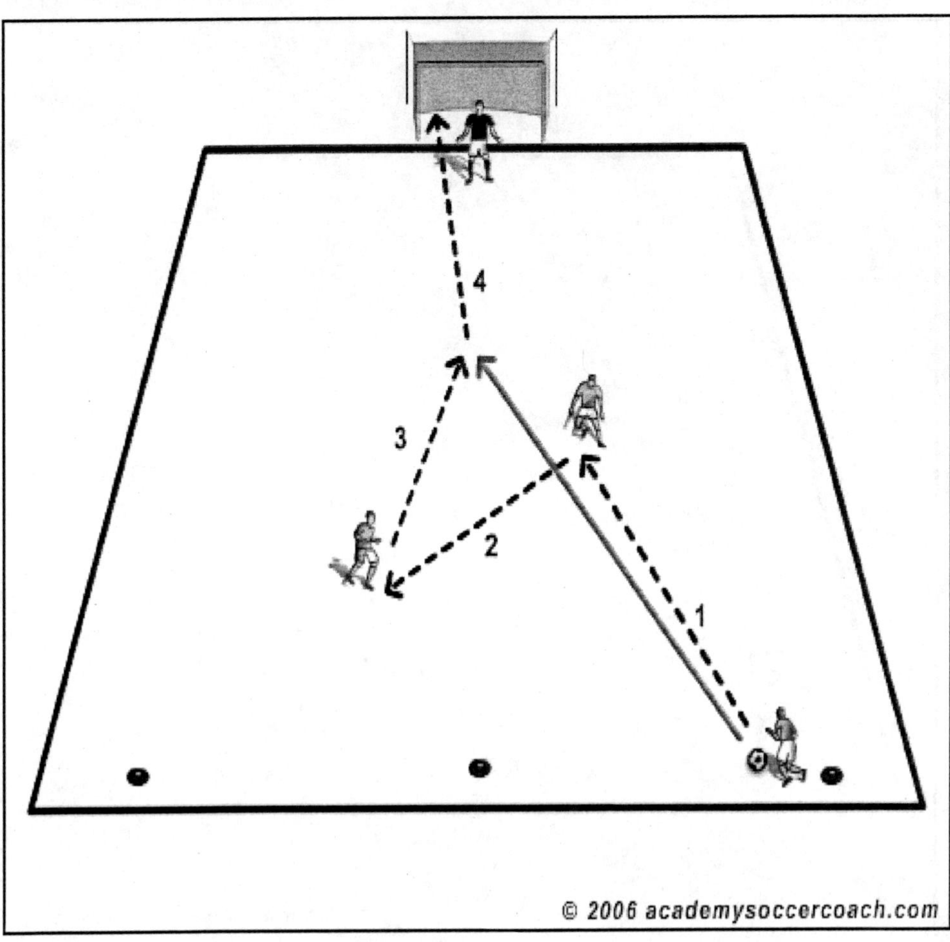

Practice 55

This practice is a progression of practice 54 and includes a 3rd player

The 3rd player now passes into player 1 and 2 who must combine with each other. After passing, player 3 now makes a run to receive a through pass in order to shoot at goal

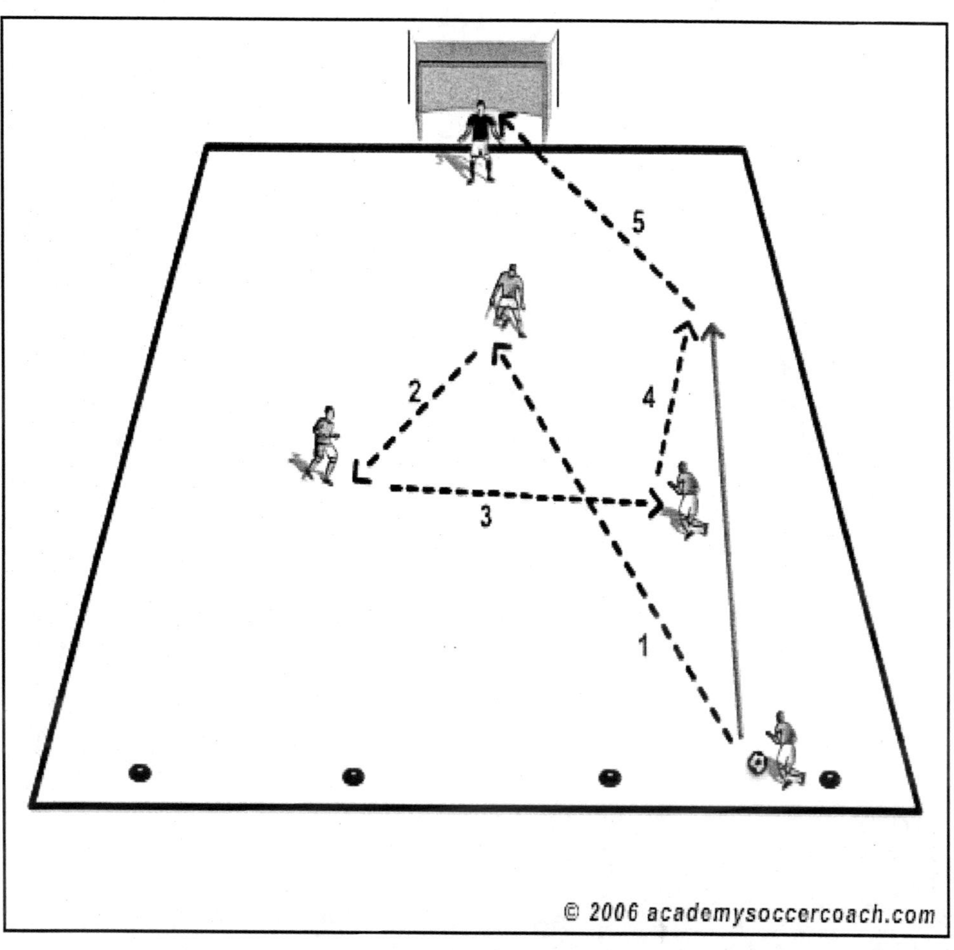

Practice 56

This practice is a progression of practices 54 and 55 and includes four players

Player 4 must now pass into players 1,2 and 3 who combine with each other
After passing, player 4 makes a run in order to receive a through pass in order to shoot at goal

If player 4 ends up in a wide area then he must improvise and cross the ball for the other players

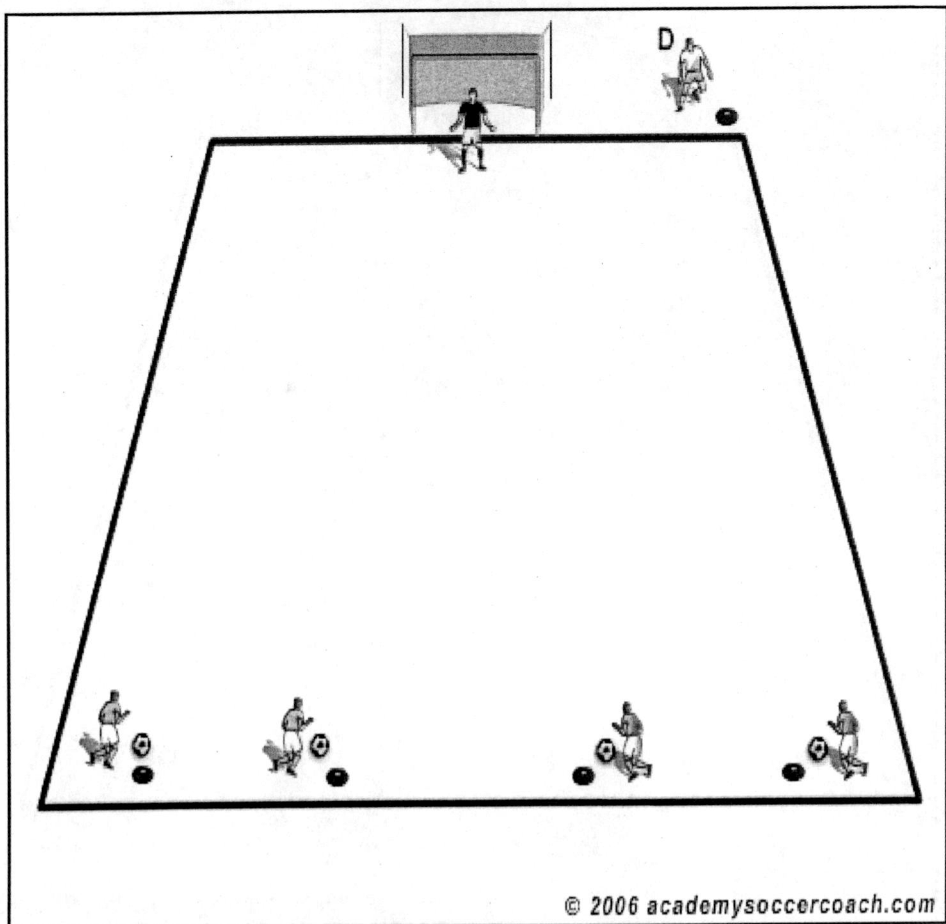

Practice 57

The defending player starts the practice by running out and calling the name of his opponent. The player called quickly dribbles onto the pitch and plays a 1v1 against the defender

Once this attack is completed, the attacker becomes the new defender and now calls out the name of a new opponent. The original defender collects a ball and waits to be called

The game continues for a set time period

Practice 58

This practice is a progression of practice 57

The defender now races out and calls the name of the opponent
After the 1v1 game is completed,
The defender now calls out the name of a team mate.
The defender and new team mate now attack 2v1 against the original attacker.
Once this 2v1 game is completed the original attacker calls out the name of a team mate
Now a 2v2 games commences
Finally the last player left is given the freedom to call two names of the team mates he would like
To attack with and a 3v2 game commences.

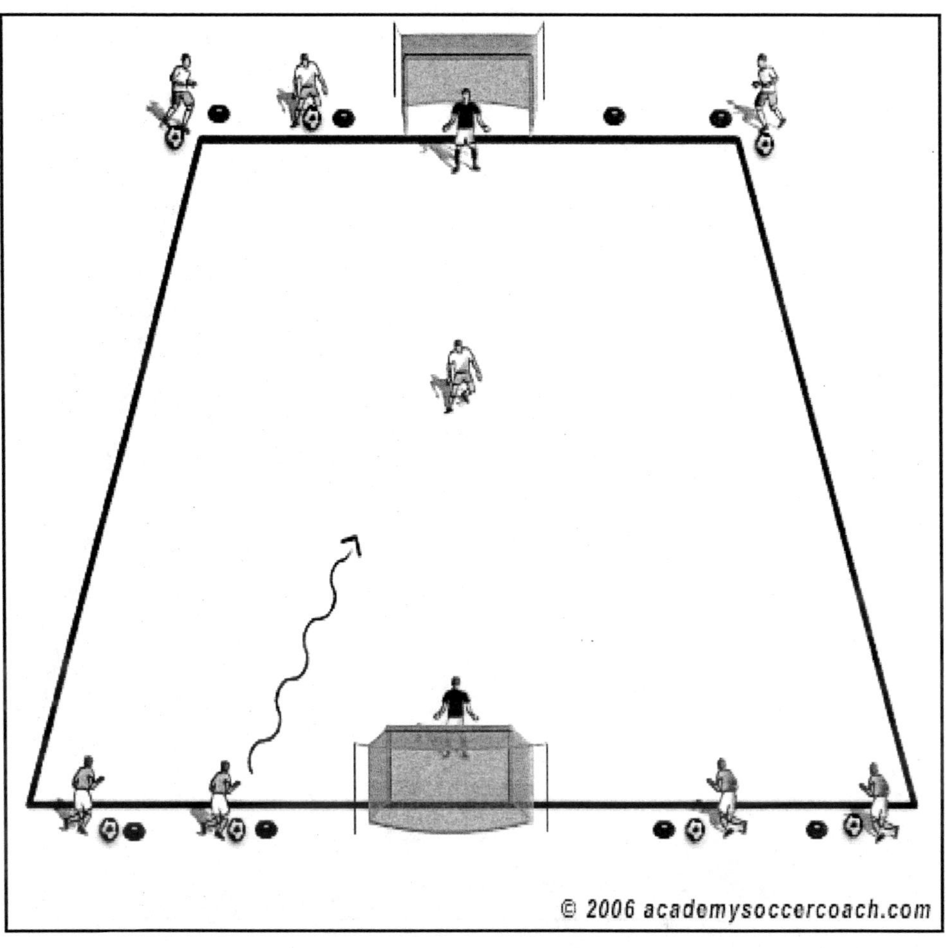

Practice 59

Two teams
Two keepers

This game is a continuous attack and defend game. on each turn the defender chooses the Player that they are going to challenge to a 1v1 game.

After having a turn as the attacker,
you must quickly react and then choose an opponent on the opposite team.
the only rule in the game is that the defender must choose a different player on each turn.

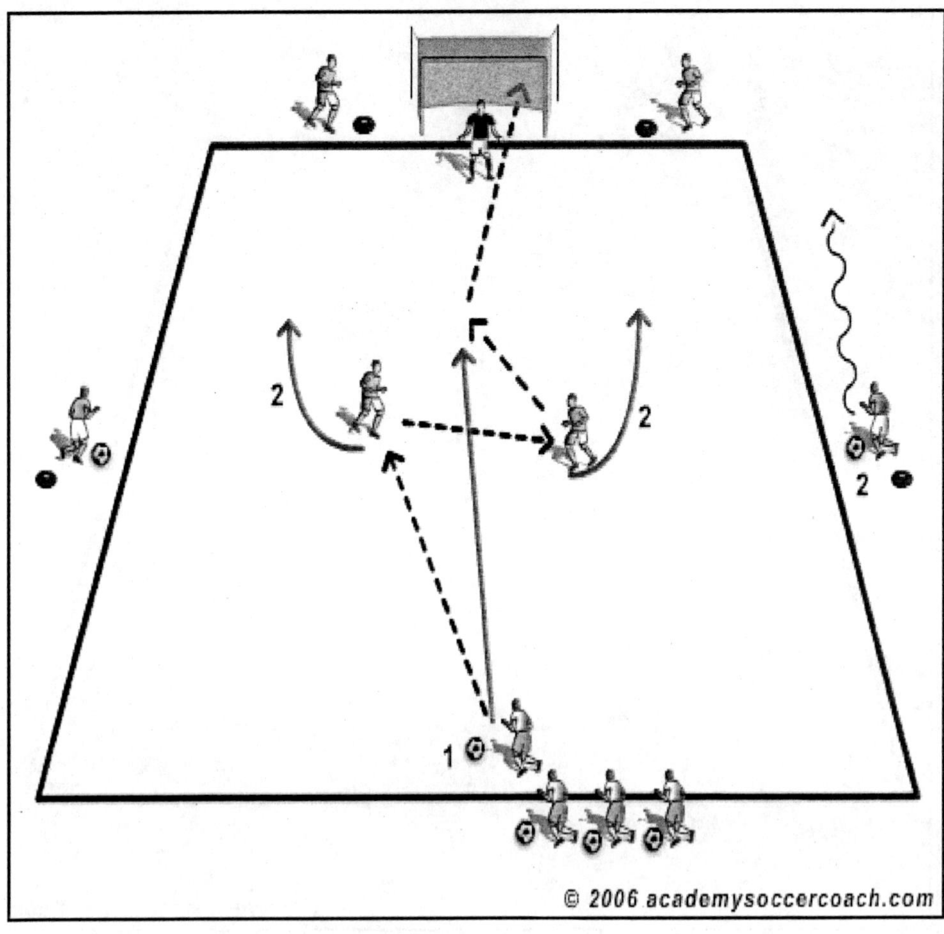

Practice 60

Player 1 must make a pass into the two forwards (players 2)
The two forwards must combine and then play a through ball to player 1
Player 1 now takes a shot at goal

Immediately after this ball is played, the coach calls “left” or “right”
The wide player called must now dribble down the line and make a cross into the box
The two forwards must now attempt to lose player 1 and score a goal

For the next attack,
Two new forwards enter the pitch
Player 1 takes the place of the wide player
The wide player joins the line to become player 1

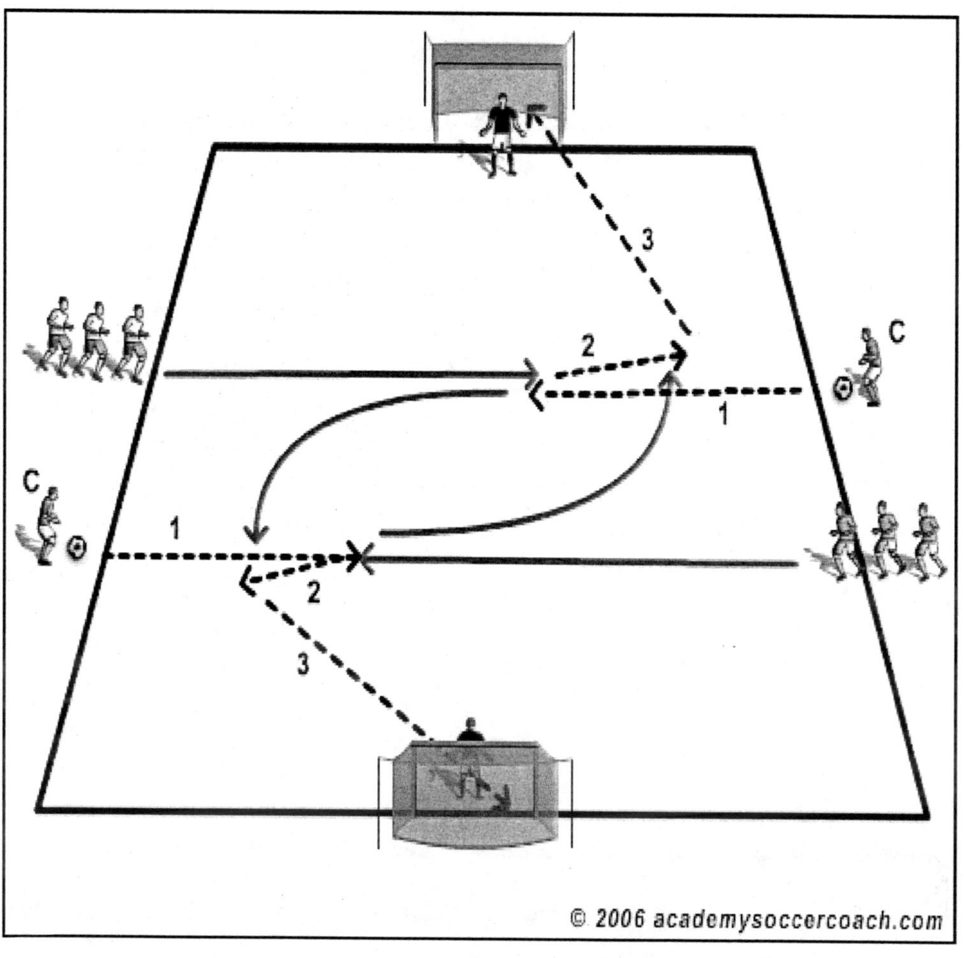

Practice 61

Both groups work at the same time

The coaches make a pass across the pitch and towards the player
The player make a wall pass into space and then spin to get the opposite ball
The players both shoot on goal 1st time .

<u>Practice 62</u>

The central player makes a pass out to the wide player
The wide player sets the ball back to the full back
The full back now plays a pass into the centre forward
The centre forward now plays the ball down the line for the wide player to run after
The wide player now crosses for the two forwards to score.

For the next attack
The central player becomes the full back
The full back becomes the wide player
The wide player becomes the forward on their side of the pitch
The forward returns to the beginning and waits to become a central midfielder

*Alternate, one attack on the left side and one attack on the right side of the pitch

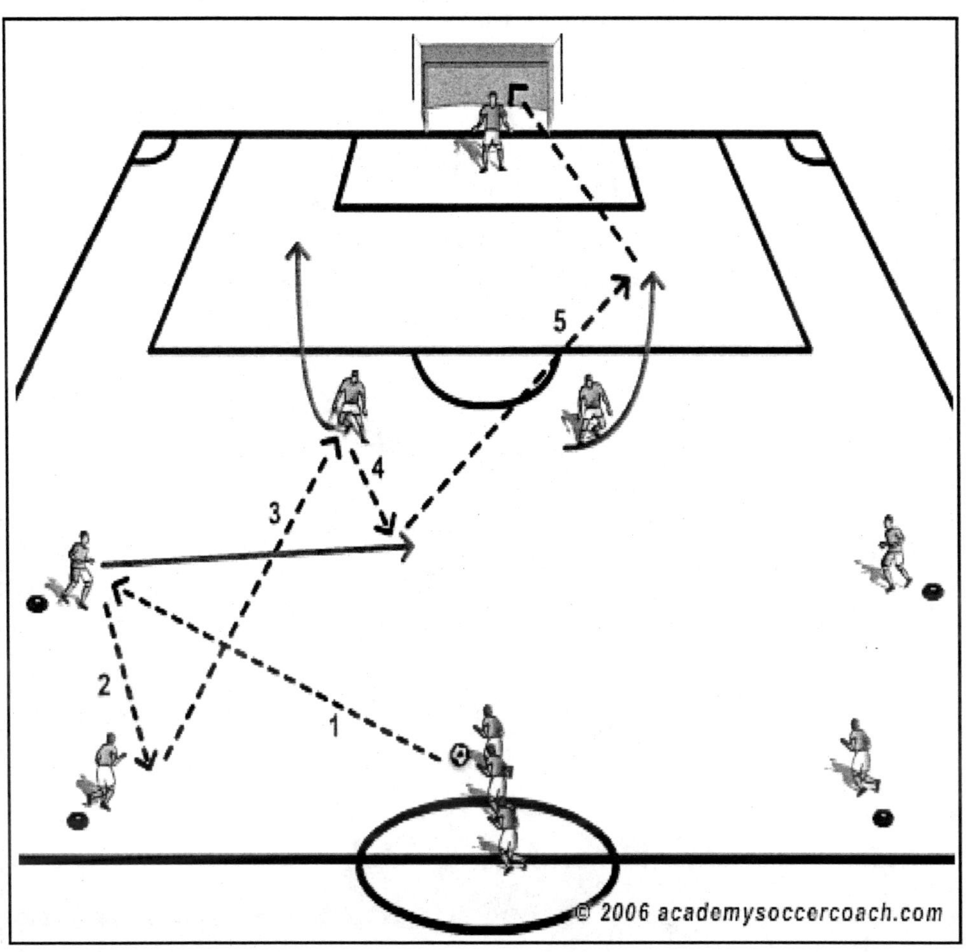

Practice 63

The central player passes to the wide player
The wide player sets back to the full back
The full back passes into the centre forward
The centre forward sets back to the wide player who has made a supporting run inside
The wide player now makes a through pass to the opposite centre forward to shoot

For the next attack
The central player becomes the full back
The full back becomes the wide player
The wide player becomes the shooting forward
The shooting forward returns to the beginning and waits to become a central midifelder

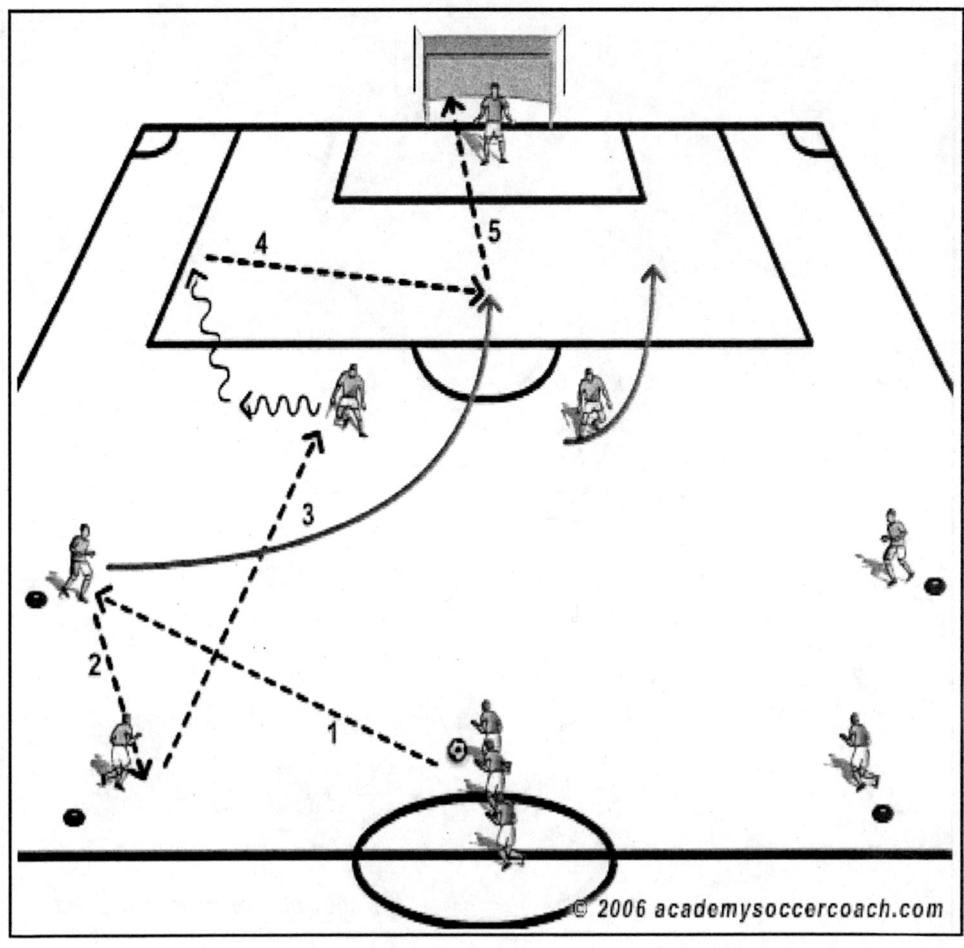

Practice 64

The central player passes to the wide player
The wide player sets the ball back to the full back
The full back passes into the centre forward.
The centre forward spins outside and into a wide area to cross
The wide player makes a run into the box with the opposite forward to score

For the next attack
The central player becomes the full back
The full back becomes the wide player
The wide player becomes the forward on their side of the pitch
The forward returns to the beginning and waits to become a central midfielder

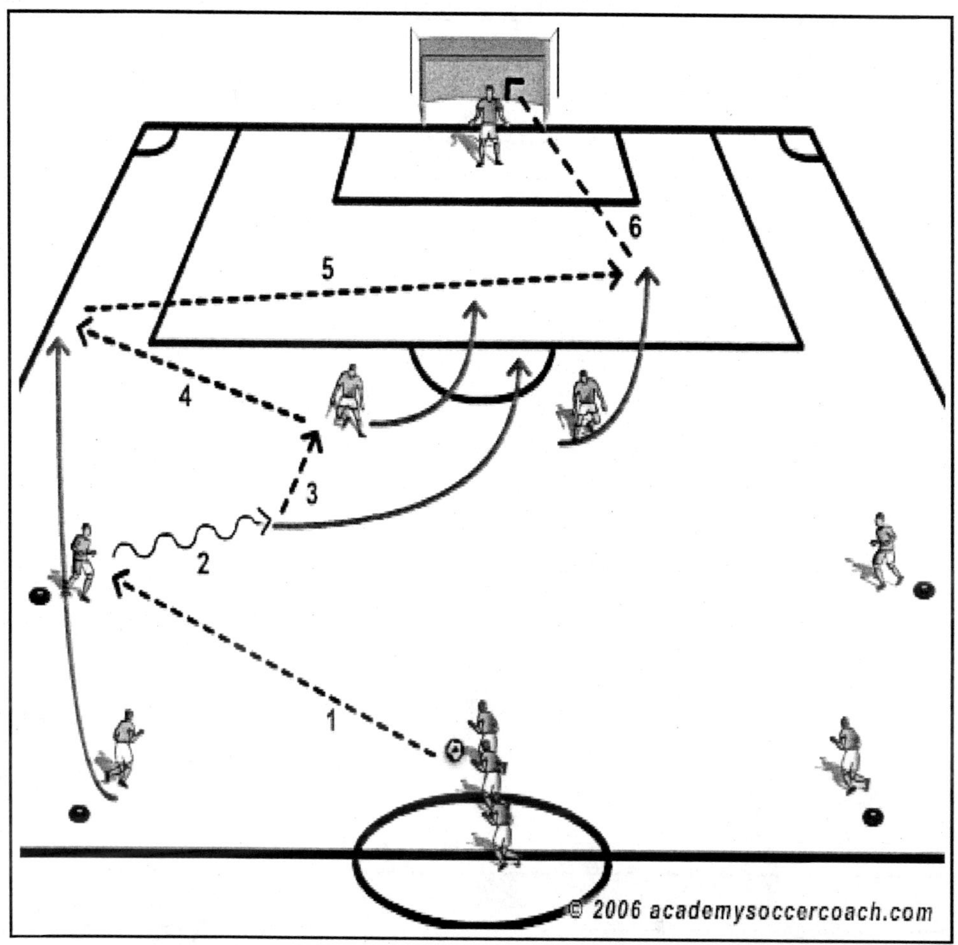

<u>Practice 65</u>

The central player passes out to the wide player
The wide player dribbles inside and passes into the forward
The forward plays a pass wide for the overlapping full back to cross
The two forwards and the wide player get into the box to score from the full backs cross

For the next attack
The central player becomes the full back
The full back becomes the wide player
The wide player becomes the forward on their side of the pitch
The forward returns to the beginning and waits to become a central midfielder

<u>Practice 66</u>

Give the players freedom of choice which practice pattern they would like to complete out of Practices 62,63,64,65. the players must be intelligent enough to react to each others decisions.

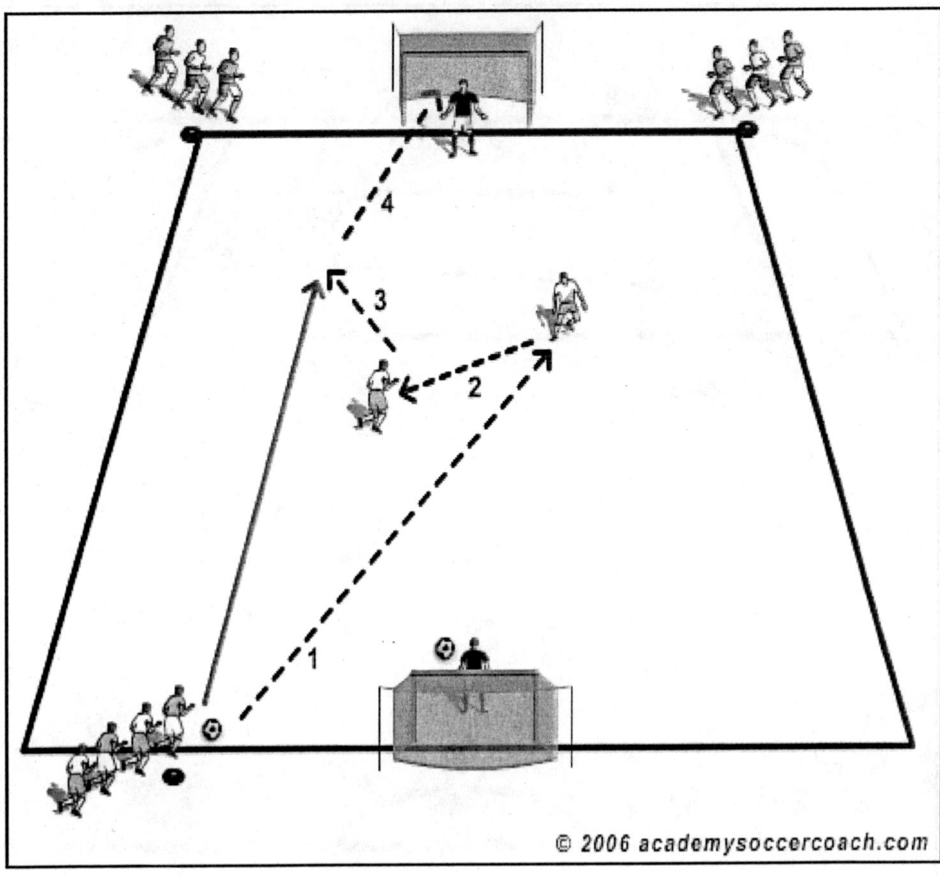

Practice 67

This practice includes a series of attacks both unopposed and opposed

To start, the first player passes into the two forwards who must combine and play a through pass, The first player makes a run to collect the through pass and then shoots on goal

Immediately after playing the through pass, the two forwards receive a pass from the opposite keeper Now the two forwards play a 2v1 against the first player. Therefore the first player must react quickly after taking the initial shot

Once the 2v1 is completed, the first player is joined by two team mates. Now the game turns Into a 3v2 attacking the opposite goal

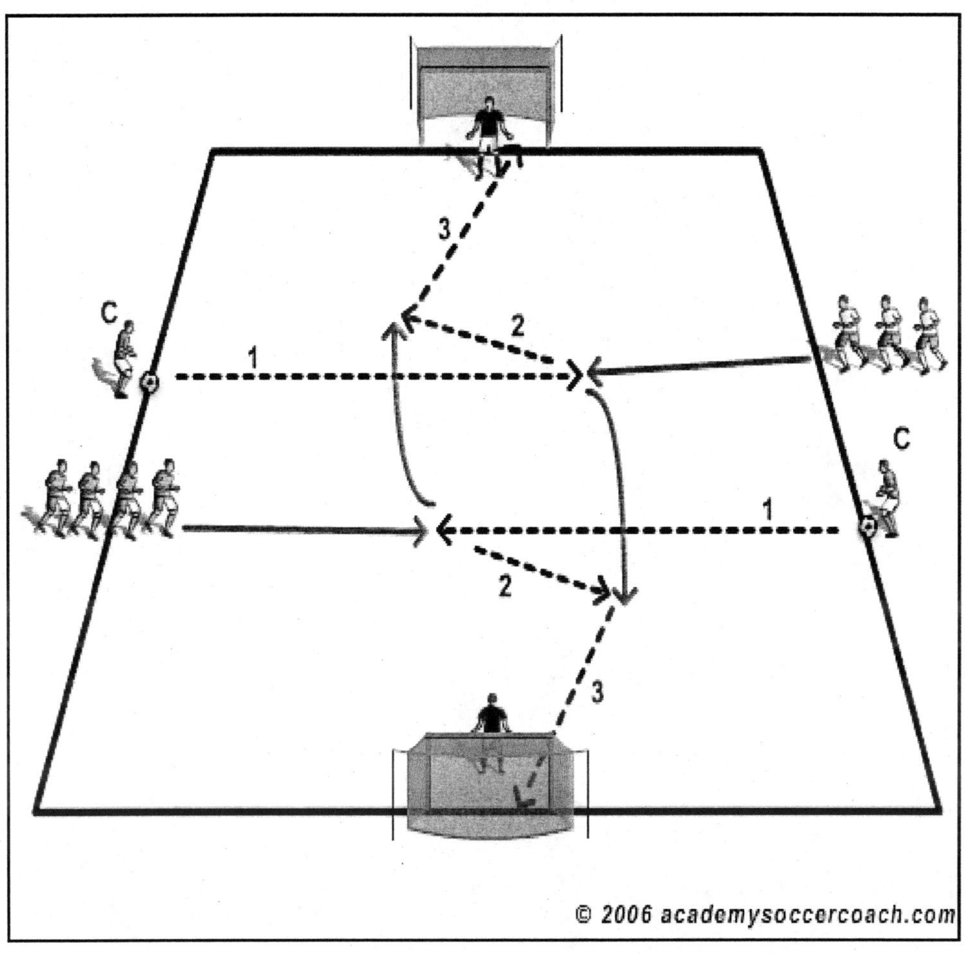

<u>Practice 68</u>

Two groups of players
Two coaches working as servers
Two keepers

To start, the coaches make passes towards the first player in the line
The player must run to meet the pass and then make a lay off into space.
Immediately after making the lay offs, both striker spin and collect the other players ball
The player are allowed one touch out of their feet and then shoot on goal

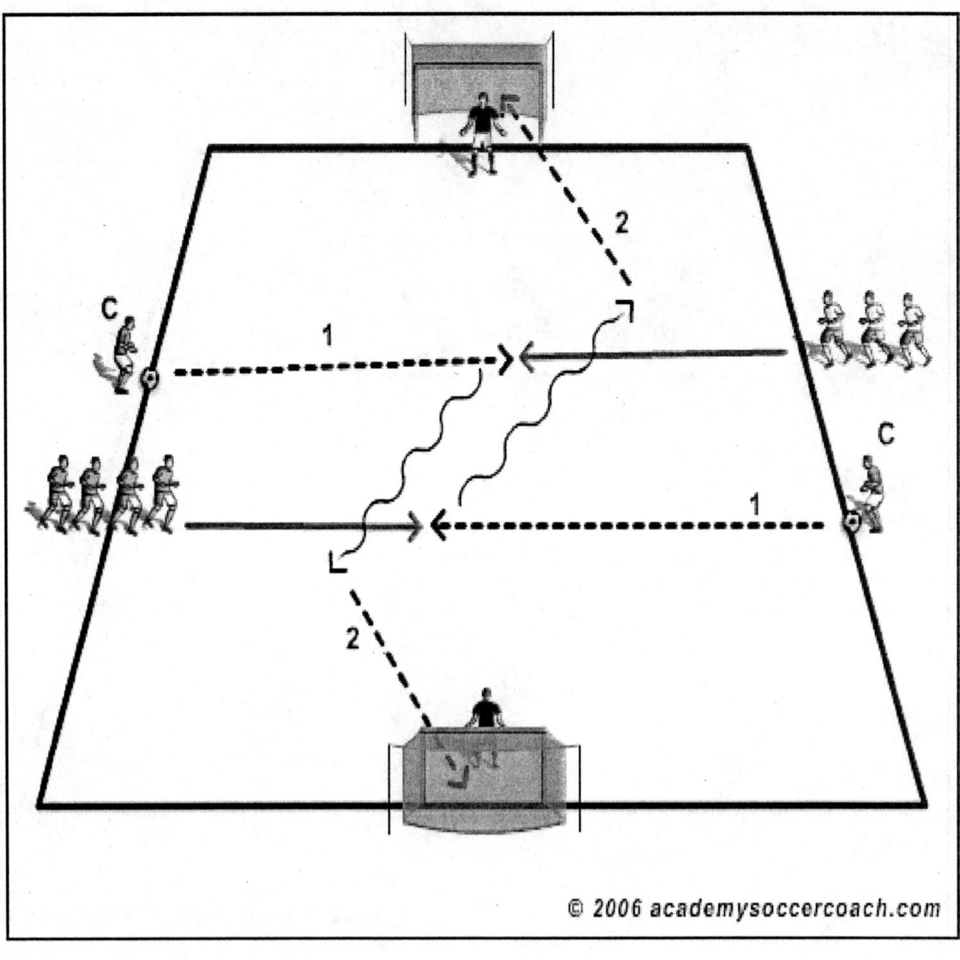

Practice 69

Two groups of players
Two coaches working as servers
Two keepers

to start, the coaches make passes towards the first player in the line
The player must run to meet the pass and then dribble across to the opposite goal
Both players then shoot on goal

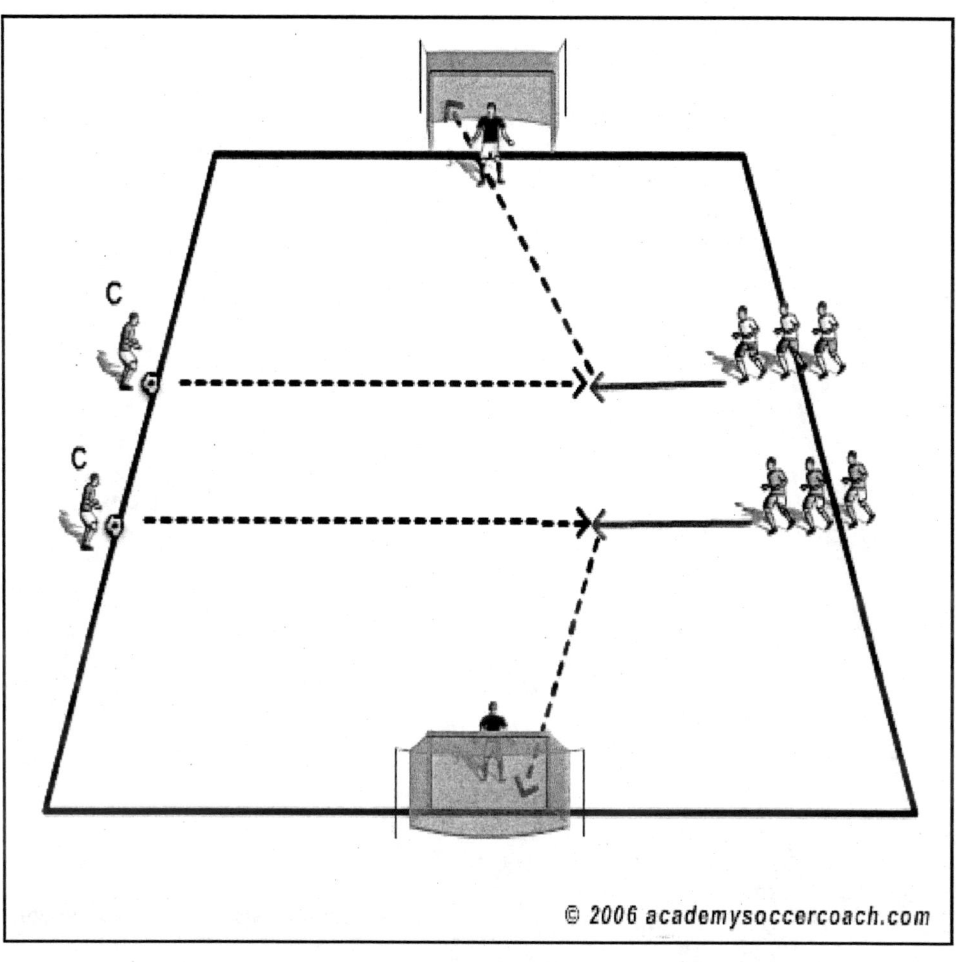

<u>Practice 70</u>

Two groups of players
Two coaches working as servers
Two keepers

to start, the coaches make passes towards the first player in the line
The player must run to meet the pass and then shoot first time across their body

For the next turn, the two players must switch sides.
This will enable players to work both their right and left foot

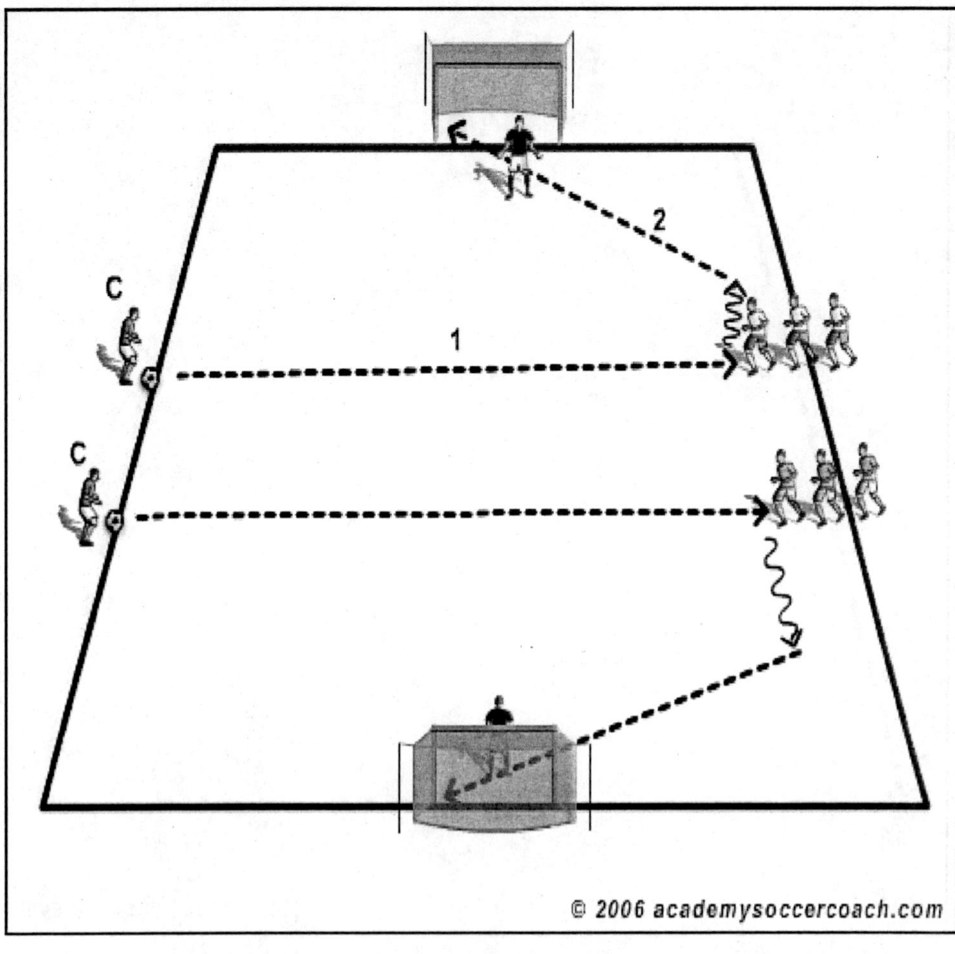

Practice 71

Two groups of players
Two coaches working as servers
Two keepers

To start, the coaches make passes towards the first player in the line
The player must run to meet the pass and then open out to shoot across the goal

For the next turn, the two players must switch sides.
This will enable players to work both their right and left foot

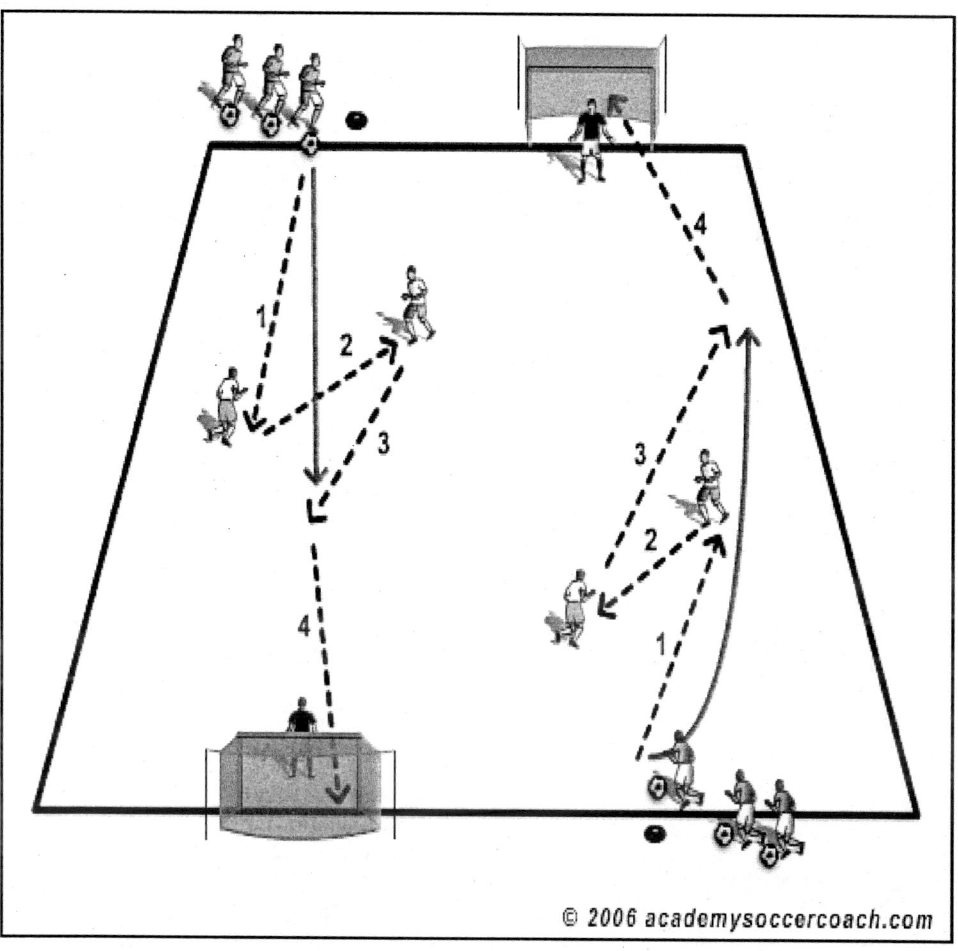

Practice 72

The player are split into pairs. Each pair take a turn as the strikers
The strikers stay on the pitch and combine to play the midfielder through to goal

The midfielders must pass into the strikers and then make a run to receive a through pass
After shooting, the strikers collect their balls and join the opposite group.

After a set time period, two new pairs of strikers are chosen by the coach

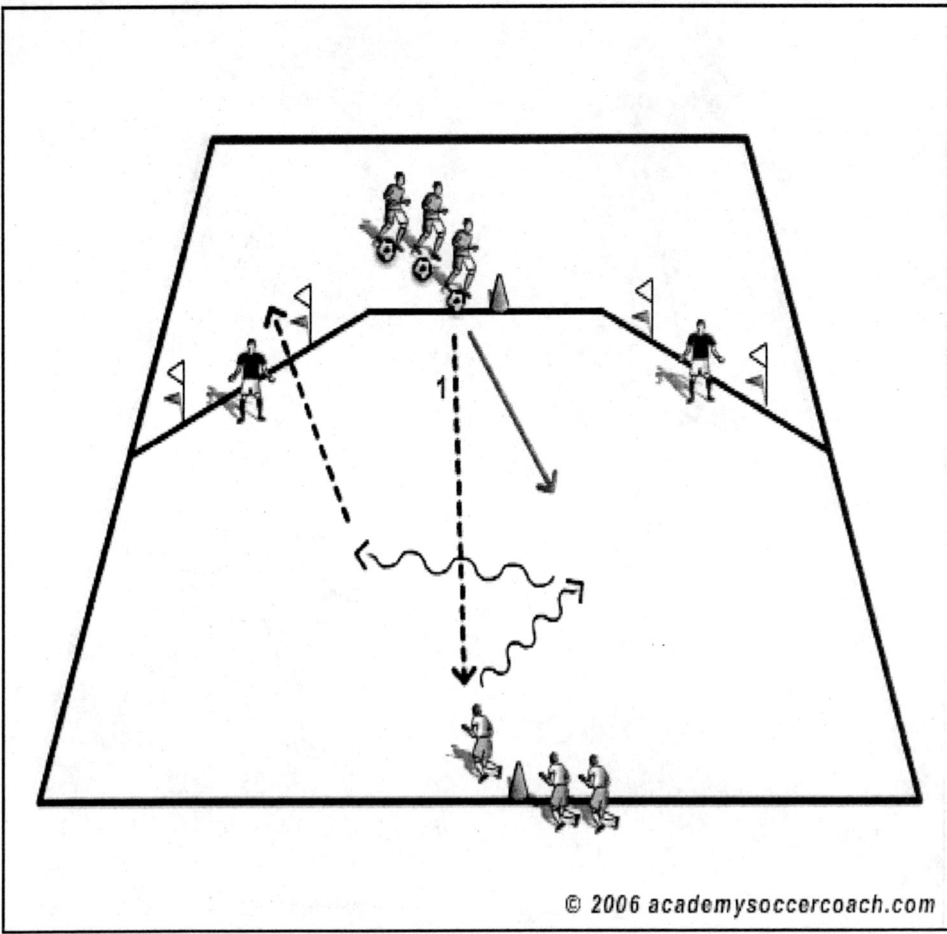

Practice 73

The defender passes into the attacker and runs to defend
The attacker must try to create space in order to shoot on goal

The attacker is allowed to score in either goal and should be encouraged to show disguise and Skill in order to lose the defender and score

The players switch positions for the next turn

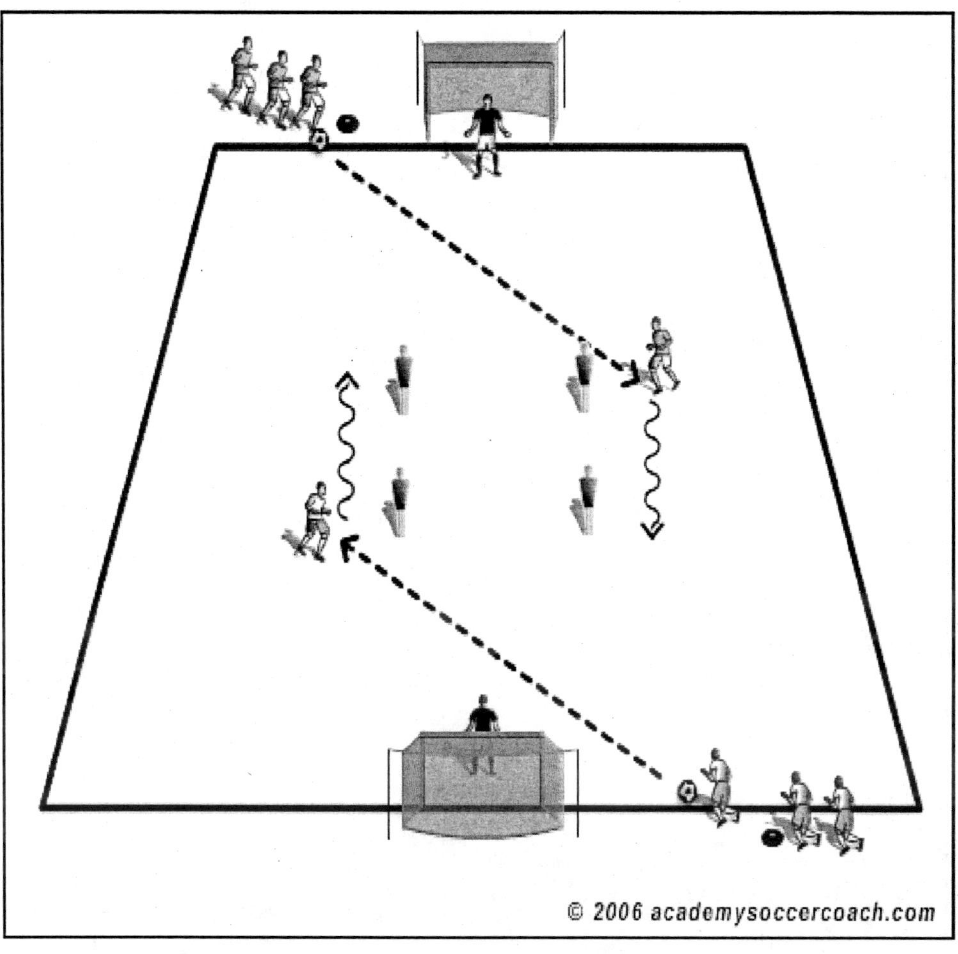

Practice 74

Both groups work at the same time

The two forwards make a movement off the mannequin in order to receive a pass
The forwards open out, and then dribble to shoot across the goal

The passing players follow their pass and become a forward

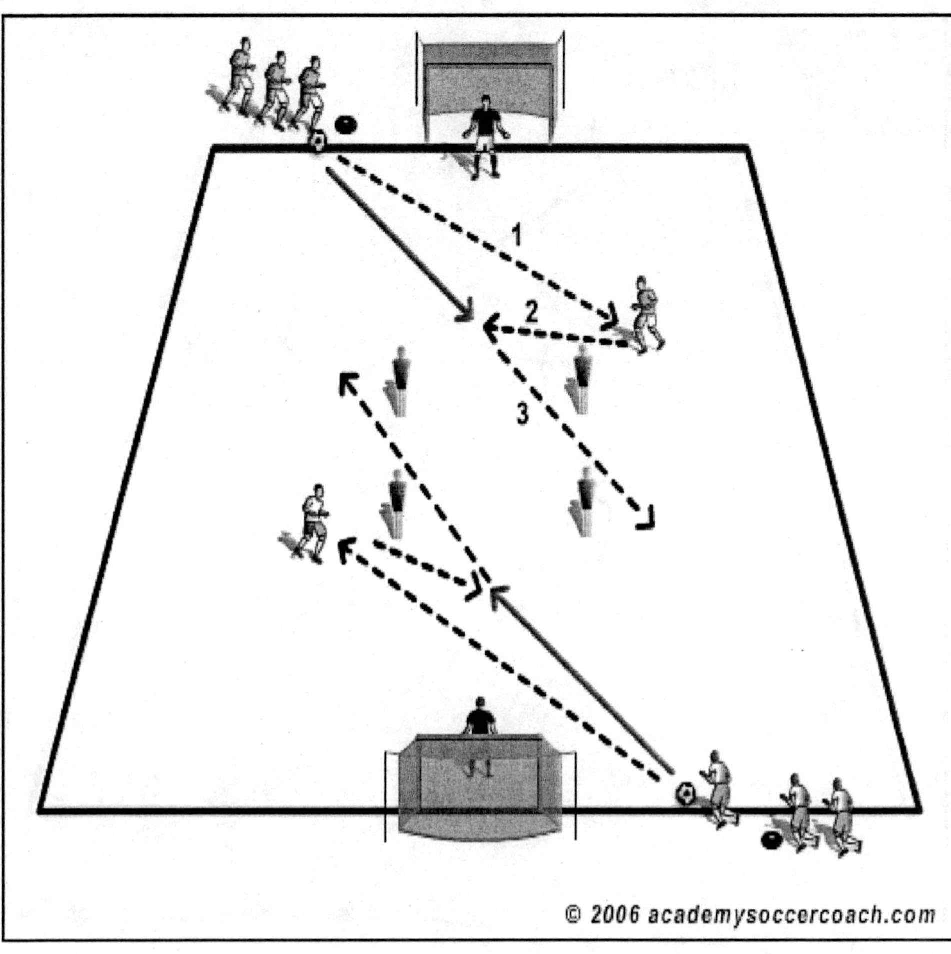

Practice 75

Both groups work at the same time

The forwards make a movement off the mannequin in order to receive a pass
The forward sets the pass to the supporting midfielder
The midfielder then returns the pass into space for the forward to spin and run after
The forward now shoots across the goal

The midfielder becomes the forward for the next turn

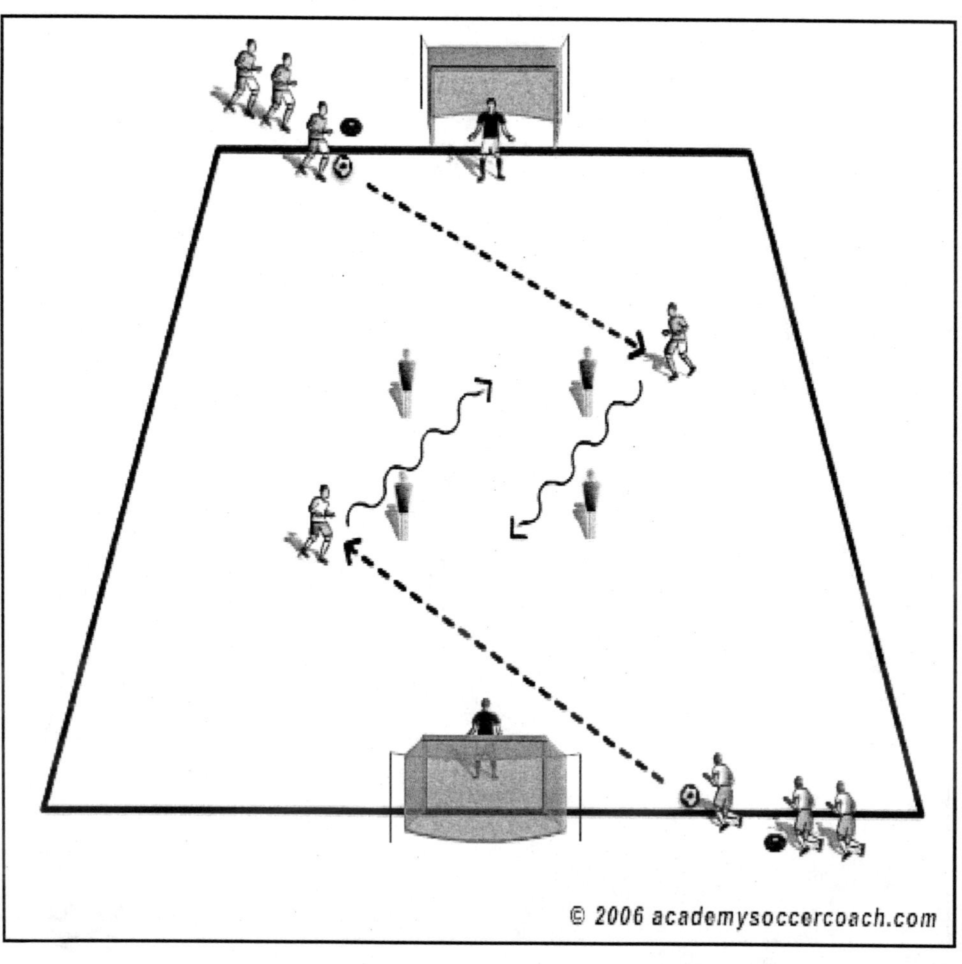

Practice 76

Both groups work at the same time

The forwards make a movement off the mannequin in order to receive a pass
The forward must let the ball run across his body
then with the first touch, go back inside the 2nd mannequin.
The forward then shoot on goal

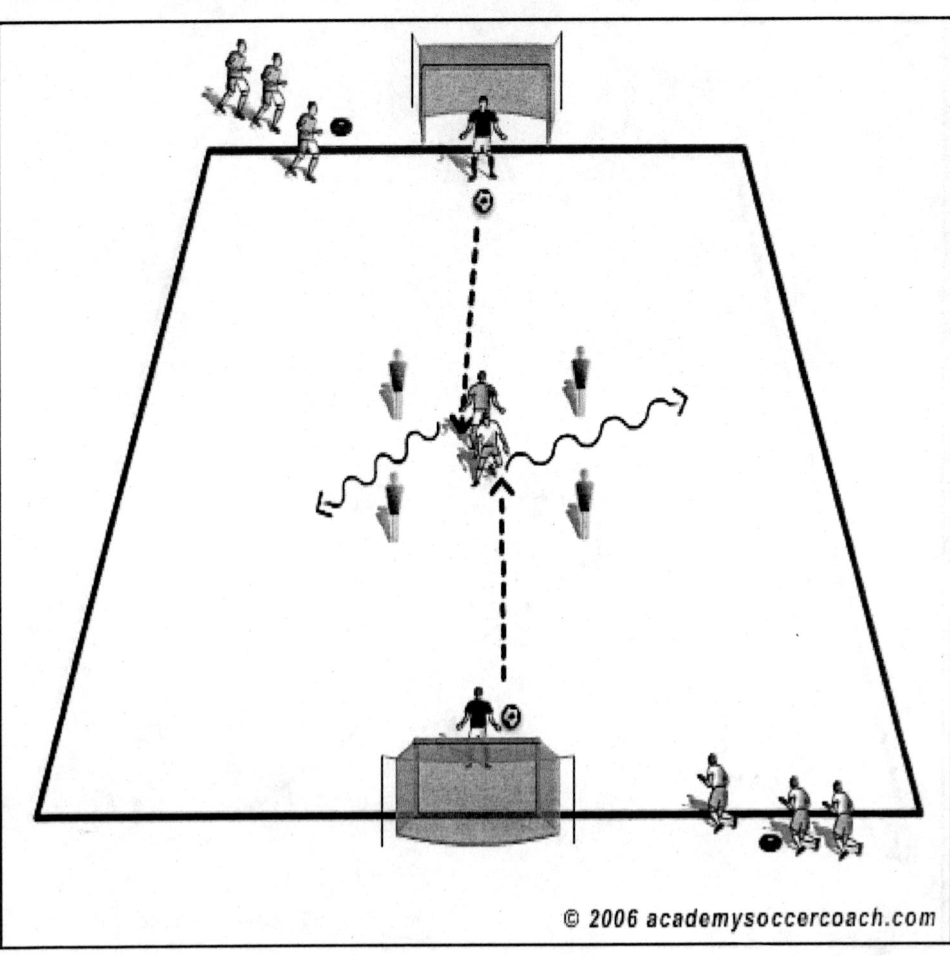

<u>Practice 77</u>

Both groups work at the same time

The keepers start the practice by rolling the ball out to the forwards.

The forwards must listen to the call from the coach (right or left)

The forward must turn in the direction called and go outside the mannequins to shoot at goal

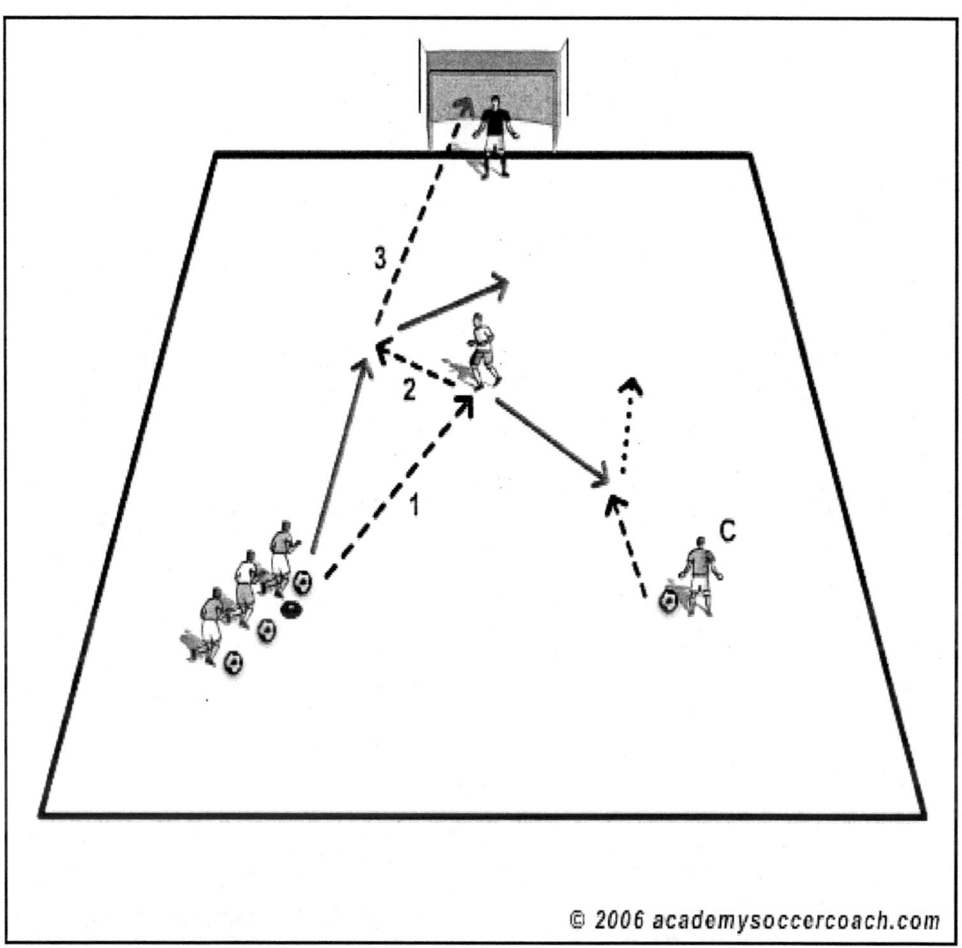

Practice 78

The key to this practice is to react to the next ball

The first player must pass into the forward and run to receive a lay off
The first player now shoots at goal

Immediately after laying the pass off, the forward must react and receive a ball from the other coach

The forward attempts to dribble and score

The first player must react and stop him from scoring

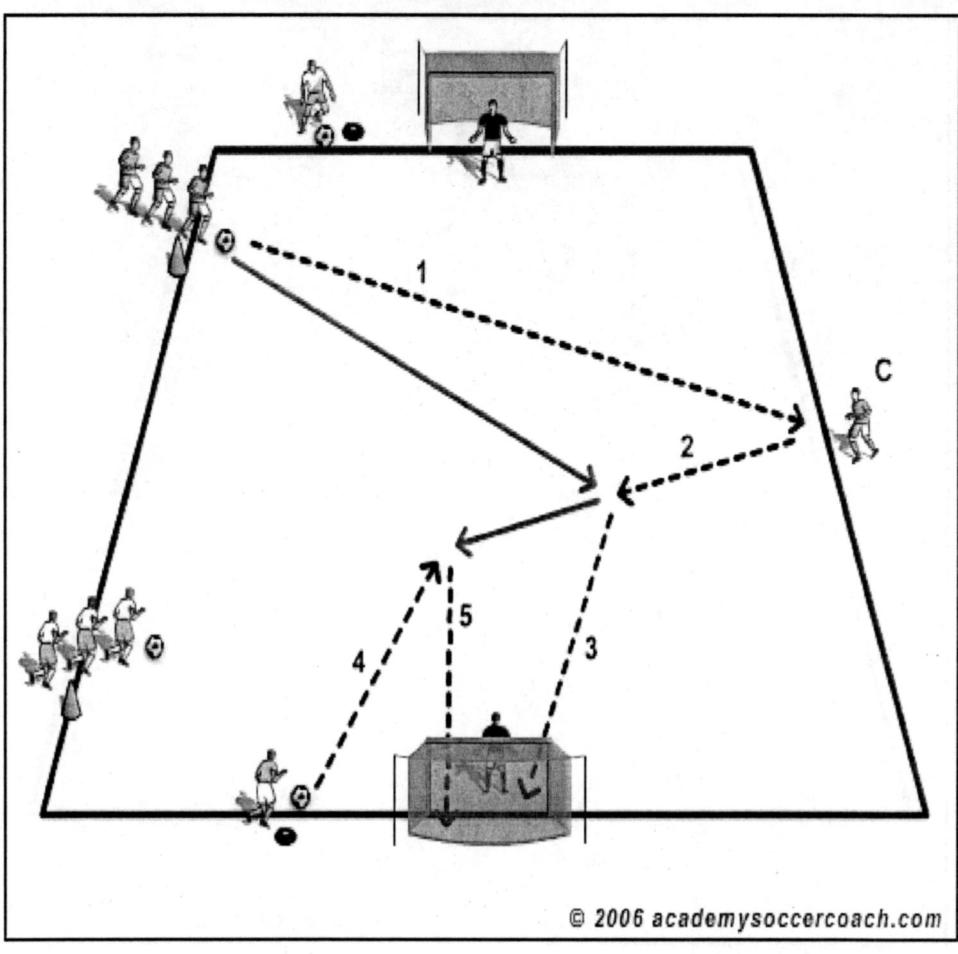

Practice 79

This practice is to work both your right and left foot
The starting player makes a long pass into the coach and runs to receive a lay off
The player now shoots with one foot (left in diagram)
After shooting, the player reacts and runs to receive a 2nd ball from the server
This time the player shoots with the other foot (right in the diagram)

After completing the circuit, the player becomes a server for the next shooter.

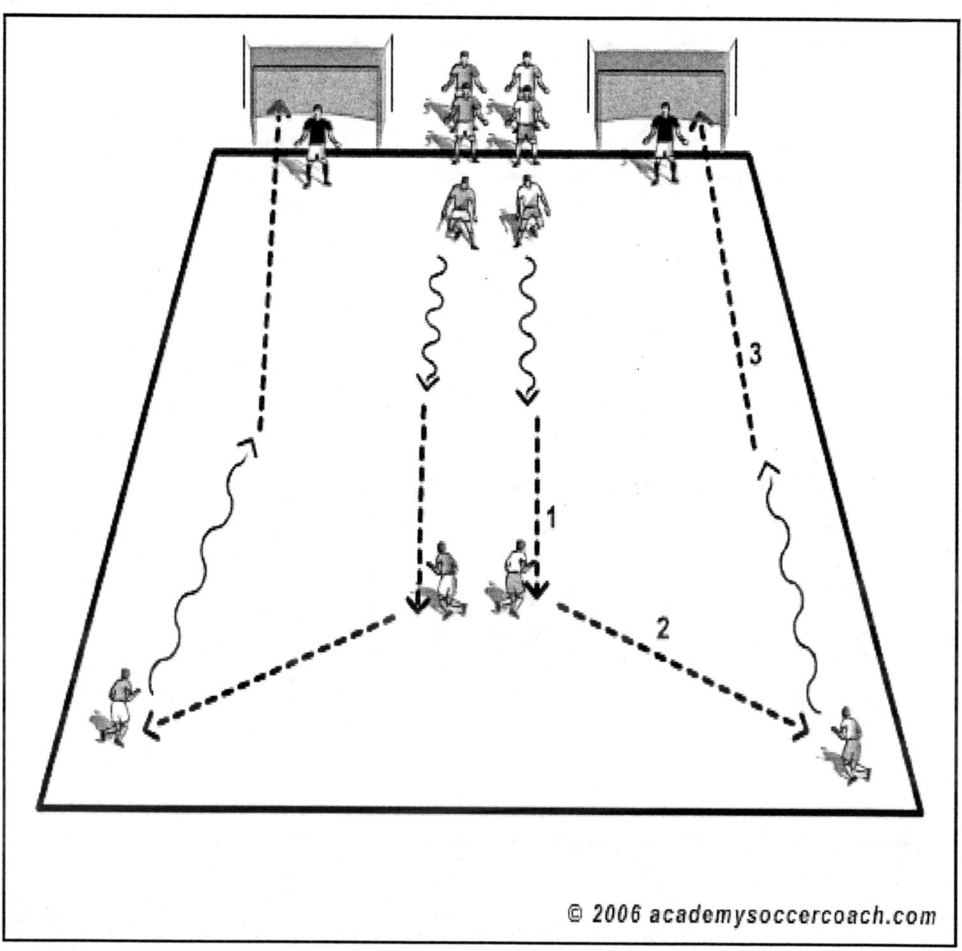

Practice 80

Both groups work at the same time
The starting player must dribble and then play a pass to player 2
Player 2 receives the ball and opens out to pass out to player 3
Player 3 then dribbles to shoot

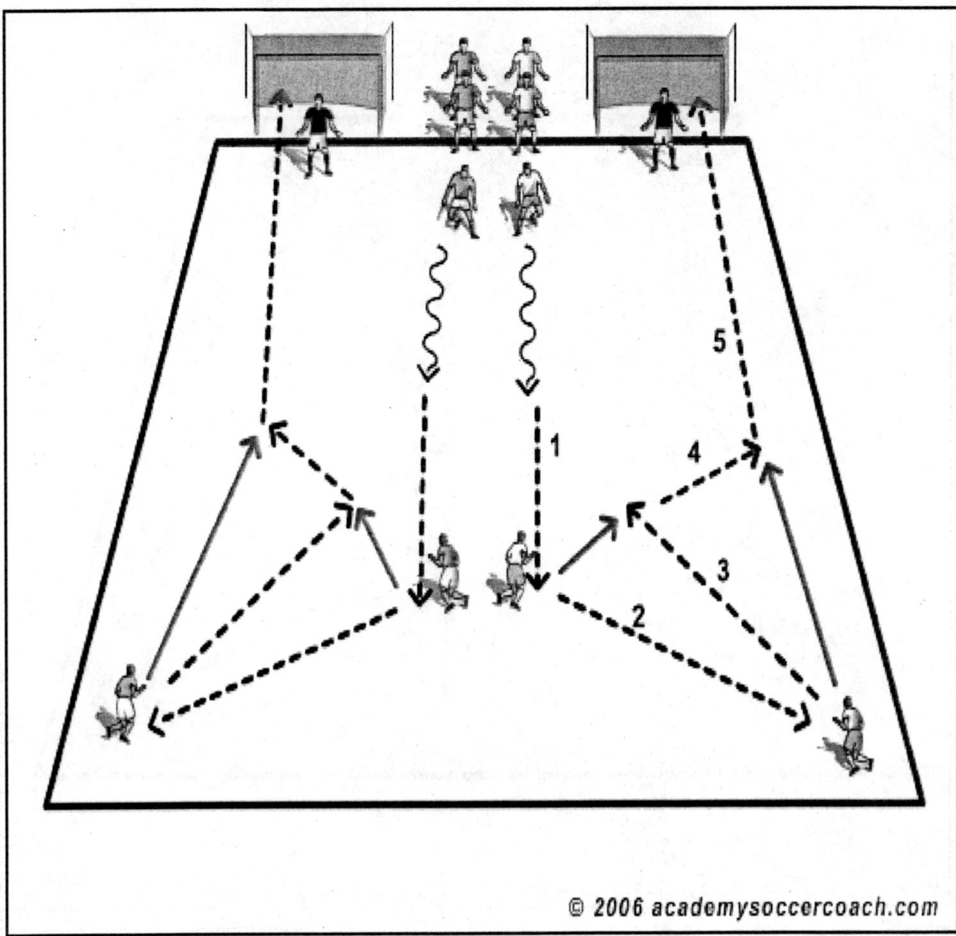

<u>Practice 81</u>

Both groups work at the same time
The starting player dribbles and then plays a pass to player 2
Player 2 receives the ball and opens out to pass out to player 3
Player 3 now plays a one-two with player 2 and then shoots at goal

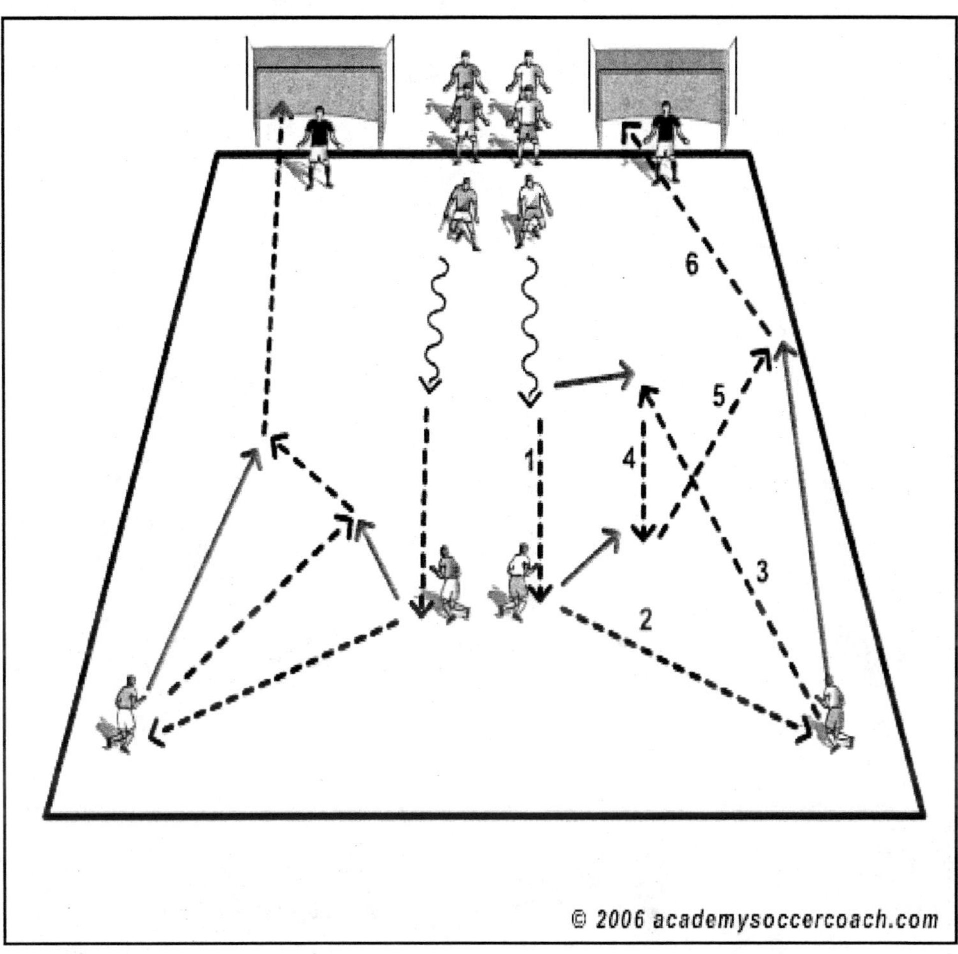

Practice 82

Both groups work at the same time
The starting player must dribble and then play a pass to player 2
Player 2 receives the ball and opens out to pass to player 3
Player 3 now plays into the starting player who has moved into a forward position
The starting player must set player 2 who plays a through pass for player 3
Player 3 now runs to receive the through pass and then he shoots at goal

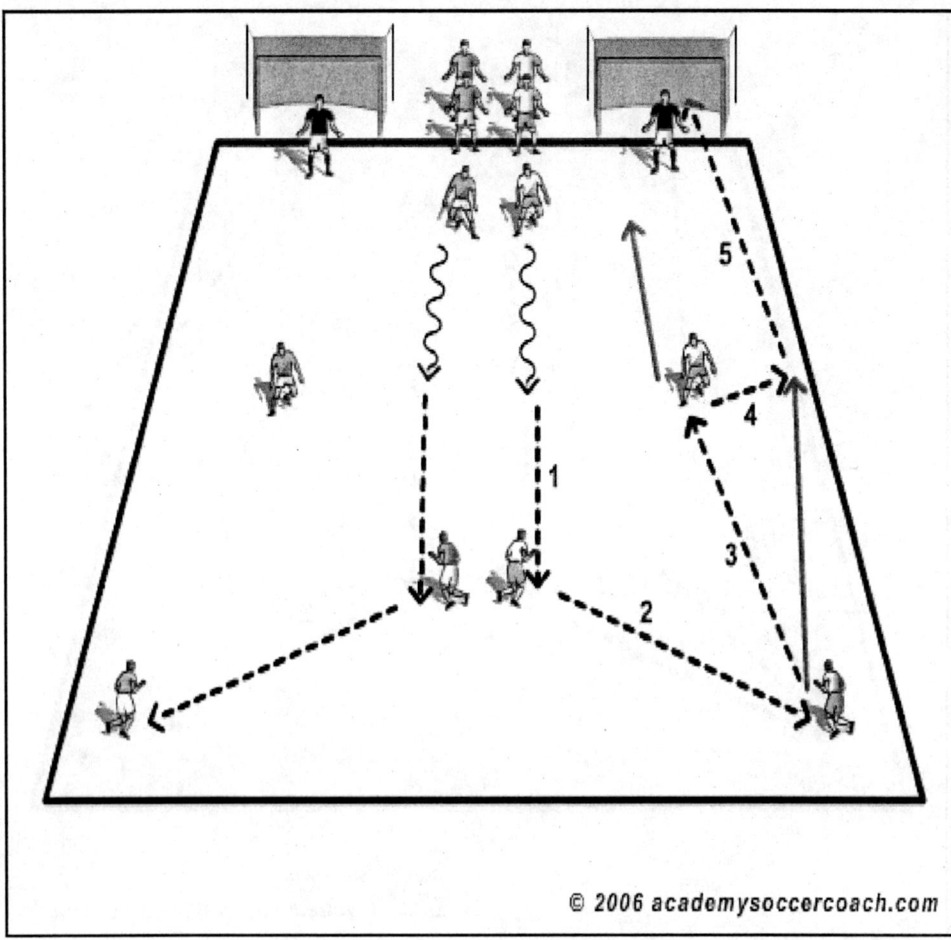

<u>Practice 83</u>

Both groups work at the same time
The starting player must dribble and then play a pass to player 2
Player 2 receives the ball and opens out to pass to player 3
Player 3 now plays into player 4 who sets player 3 to shoot
Player 4 must now react and look for any rebounds

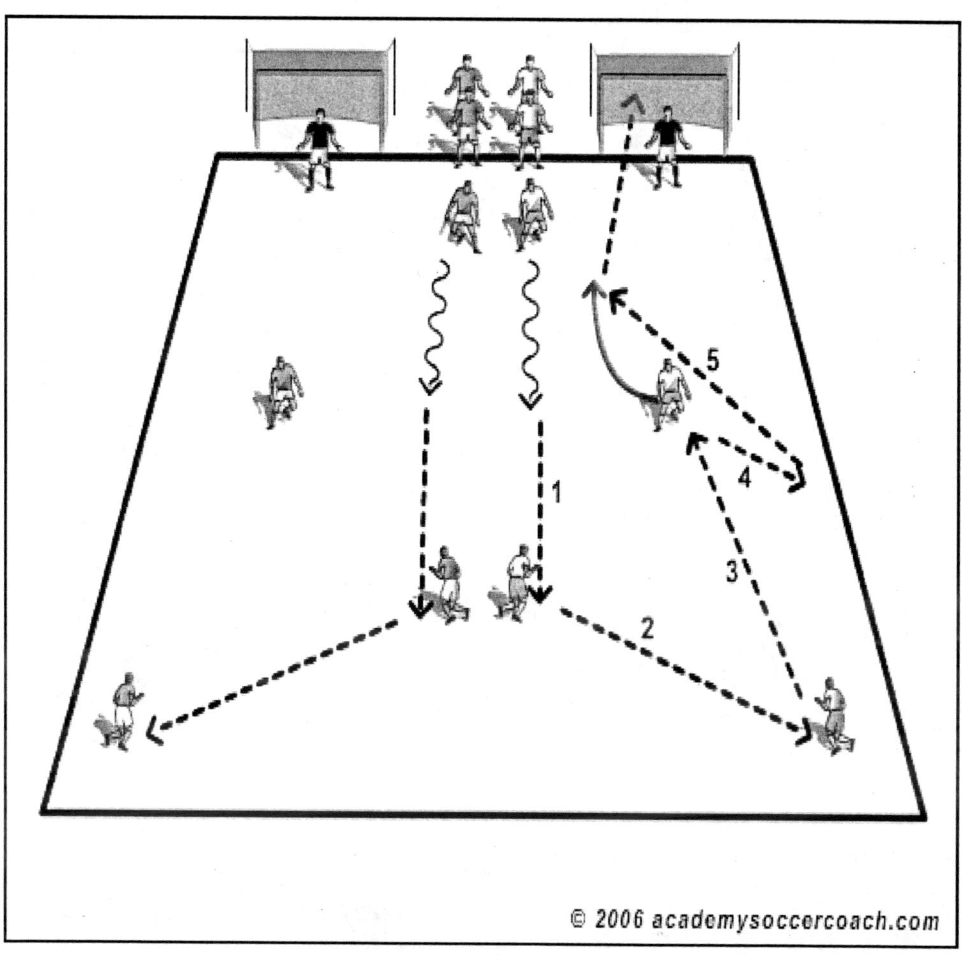

Practice 84

Both groups work at the same time
The starting player must dribble and then play a pass to player 2
Player 2 receives the ball and opens out to pass to player 3
Player 3 now plays into player 4 who sets back to player 3 and spins into space
Player 3 now plays a through pass to player 4.
Player 4 shoots at goal

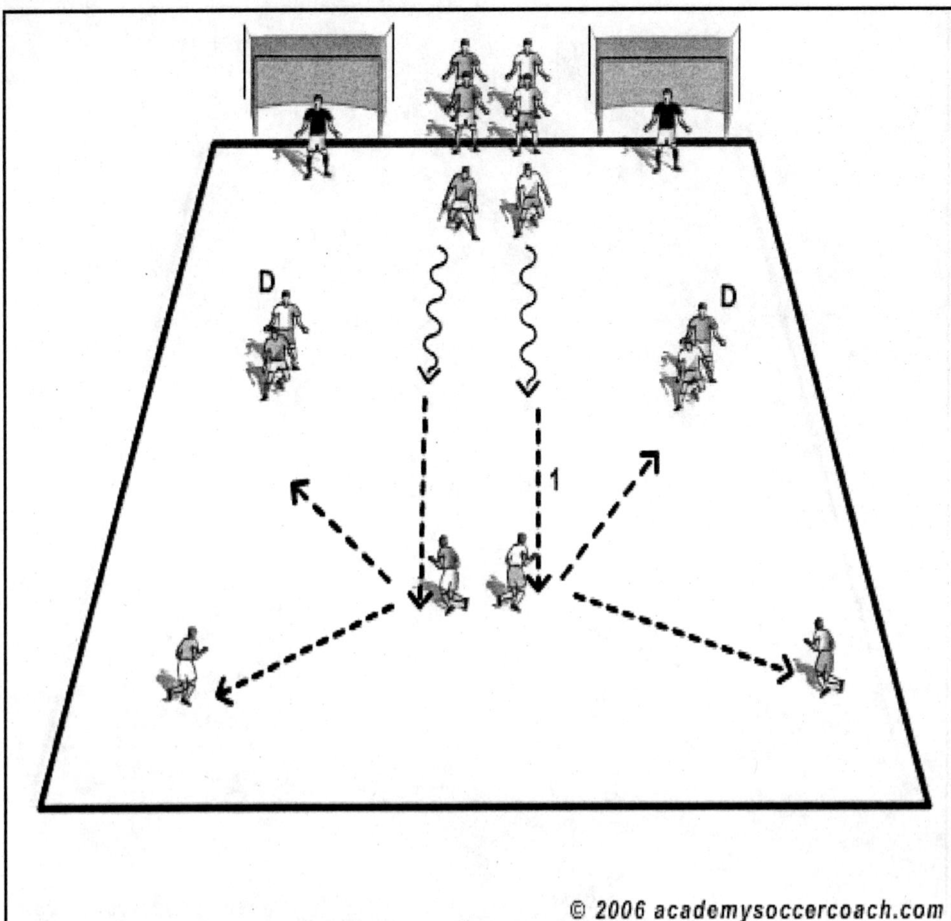

<u>Practice 85</u>

The starting player dribbles and passes to player 2
Player 2 receives the pass and can play into the forward or wide player
the wide player and forward must react to player 2's pass and attempt to score in a 2v1 situation

Each player moves to the next position

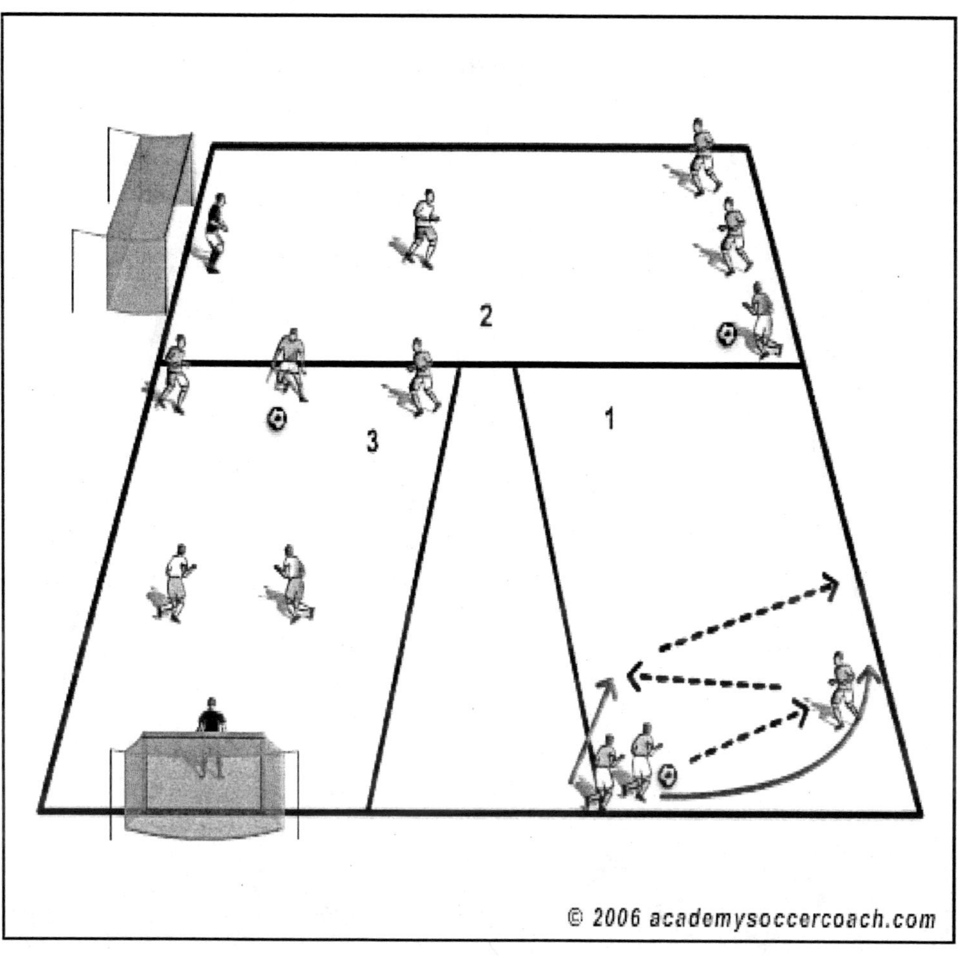

<u>Practice 86</u>

The players work in threes and have a turn at each pitch

Pitch 1 – the three players pass and overlap continuously until they reach pitch 2
Pitch 2 – the three players attempt to score in a 3v1 situation
Pitch 3 – the three players attempt to score in a 3v2 situation

The coach must ensure that each group of three players takes a turn as the defenders.

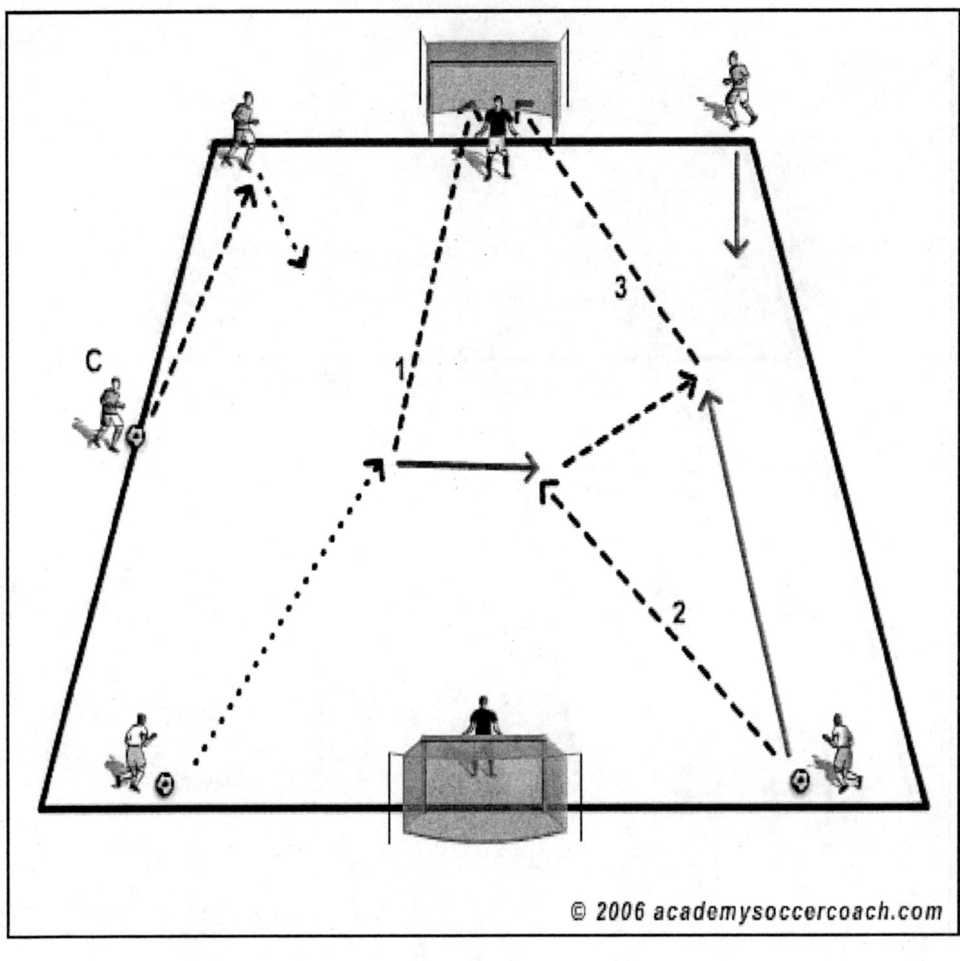

<u>Practice 87</u>

The white team work as the shooters.
The first player must dribble and shoot at goal
the 2nd player now combines with the first player and shoots at goal

The coach now passes to the grey team.
A 2v2 games commences.

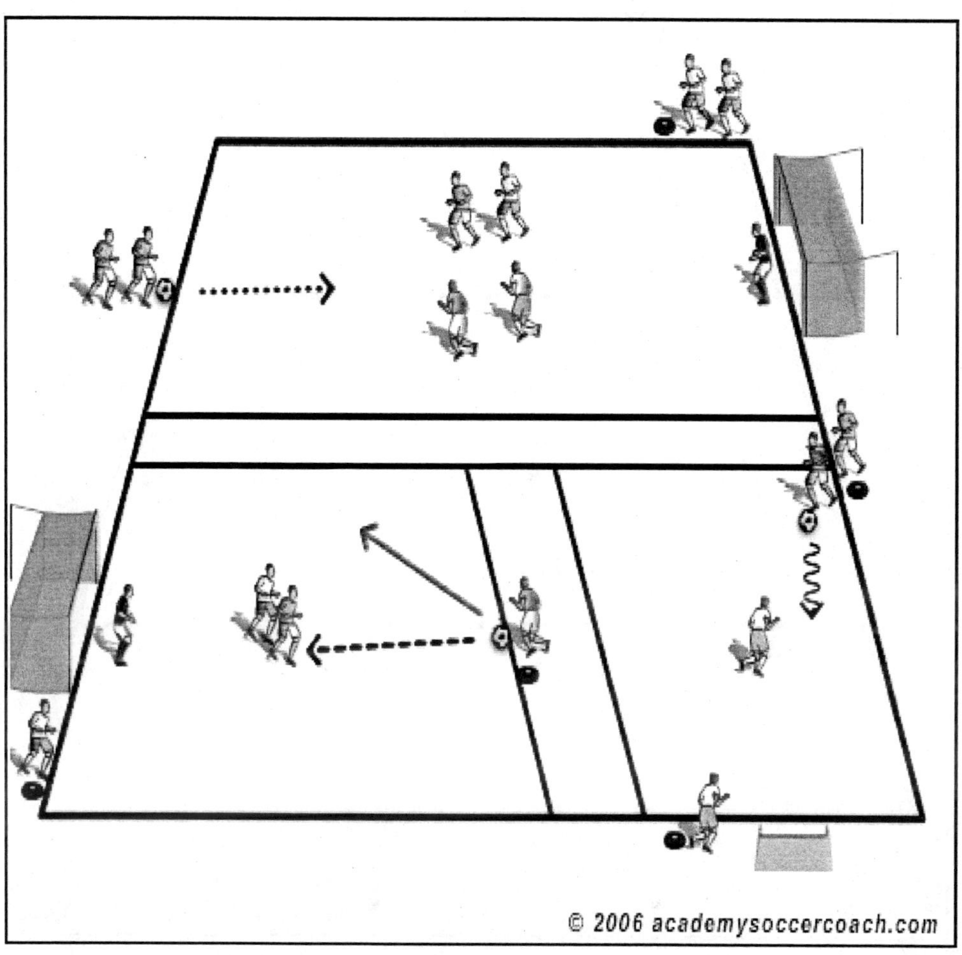

<u>Practice 88</u>
Two teams of 8 players
Three pitches

Pitch 1 – 1v1
Pitch 2 – 2v1
Pitch 3 – 3v2

All three pitches are working at the same time.
The attacking players move from pitch to pitch while the defenders stay to their own pitch

The attackers will take the following path.
Pitch 1 – dribble and attack
Pitch 2 – pass and make a supporting run
Pitch 2 – become the forward
Pitch 3 – dribble to make a 3v2
Pitch 3 – become a forward
Pitch 3 – become a forward for the 2nd time
Now rest and start at pitch 1 again.

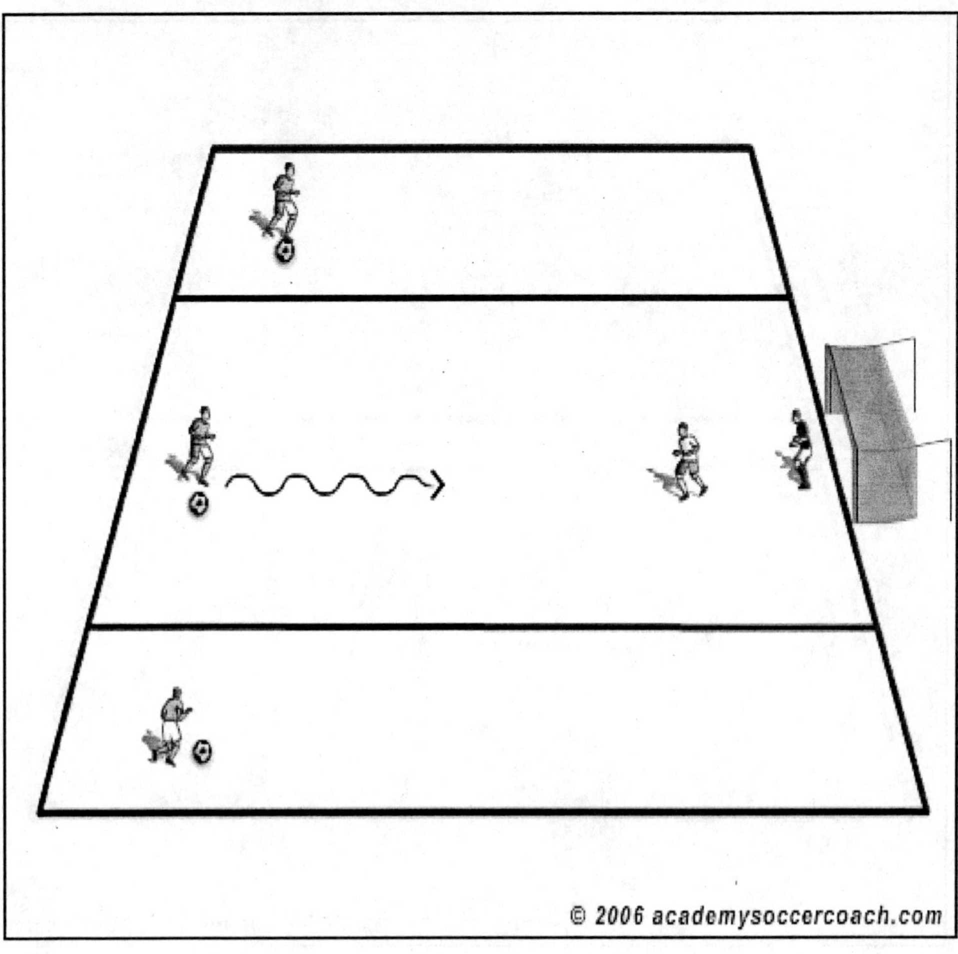

<u>Practice 89</u>

The centre forward dribbles and plays 1v1 against the defender in the central zone
Once this ball is completed
The left forward dribbles and crosses for the forward and defender to compete 1v1
Once this ball is completed
The right forward dribbles and crosses for the centre and left forward to compete 2v1 on the cross

The players rotate positions for the next attack

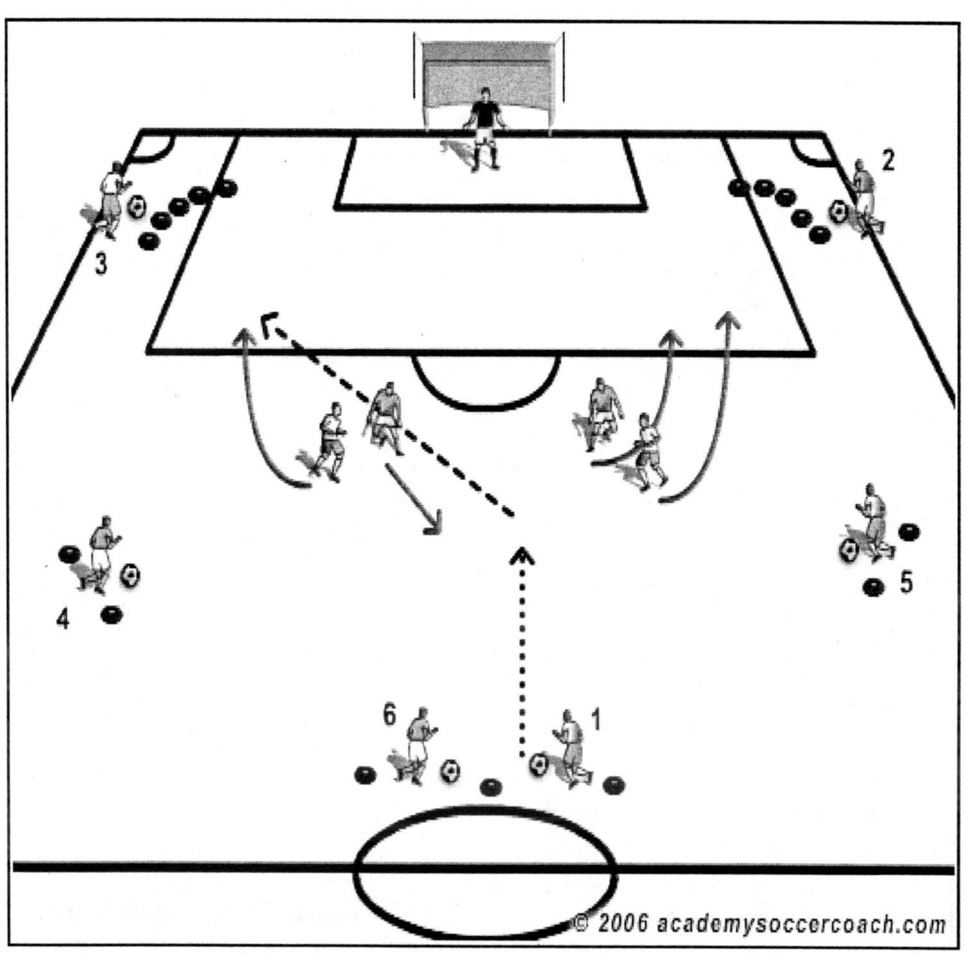

Practice 90

Each team has two players on the pitch
The other three players must spread across the stations
The teams rotate from attacking to defending

The coach calls out the number of the player who is to dribble into the area.
The game now commences in a 3v2 situation

The various positions that the players are in and where the ball is coming from will enable the players to experience various attacking situations and problems to solve

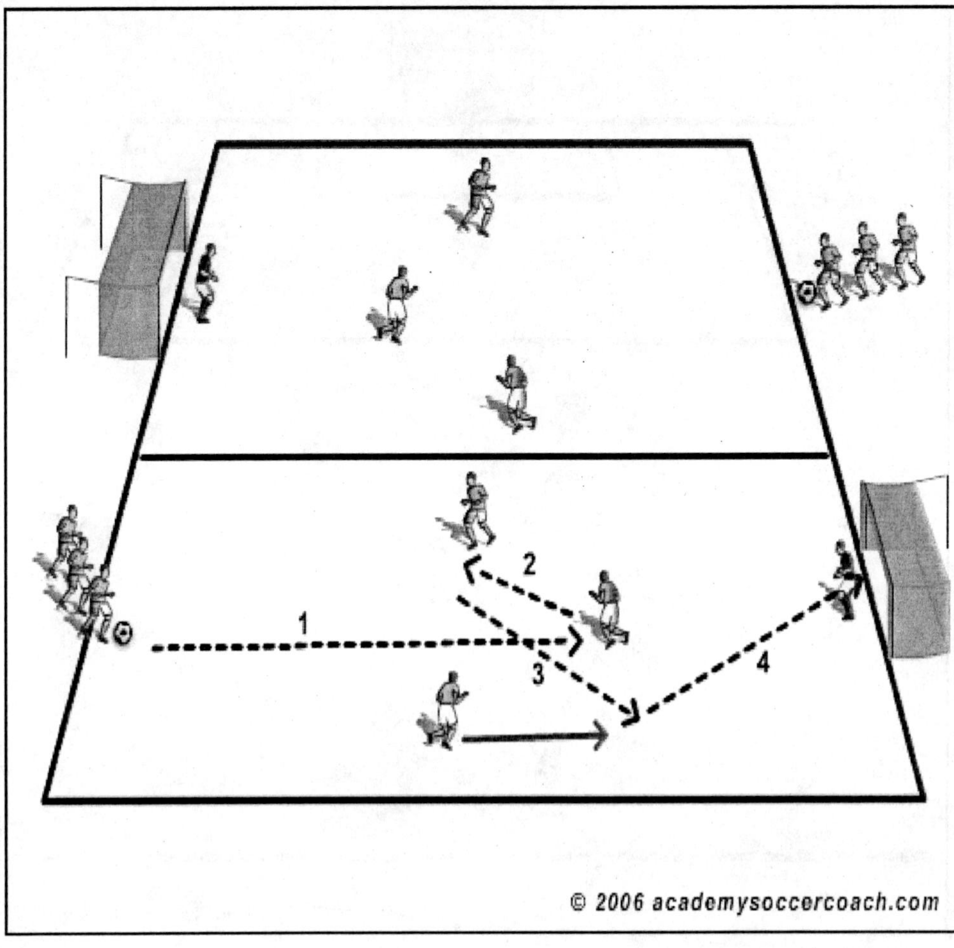

<u>Practice 91</u>

Three players start on each pitch
The rest of the players wait for the turn to pass onto the pitch

To start, the passer plays into the three forwards
The forwards must combine quickly in order to get a shot aon goal

The shooting player now collects his ball and joins the opposite group.
The passing player now becomes a forward

Both groups work at the same time

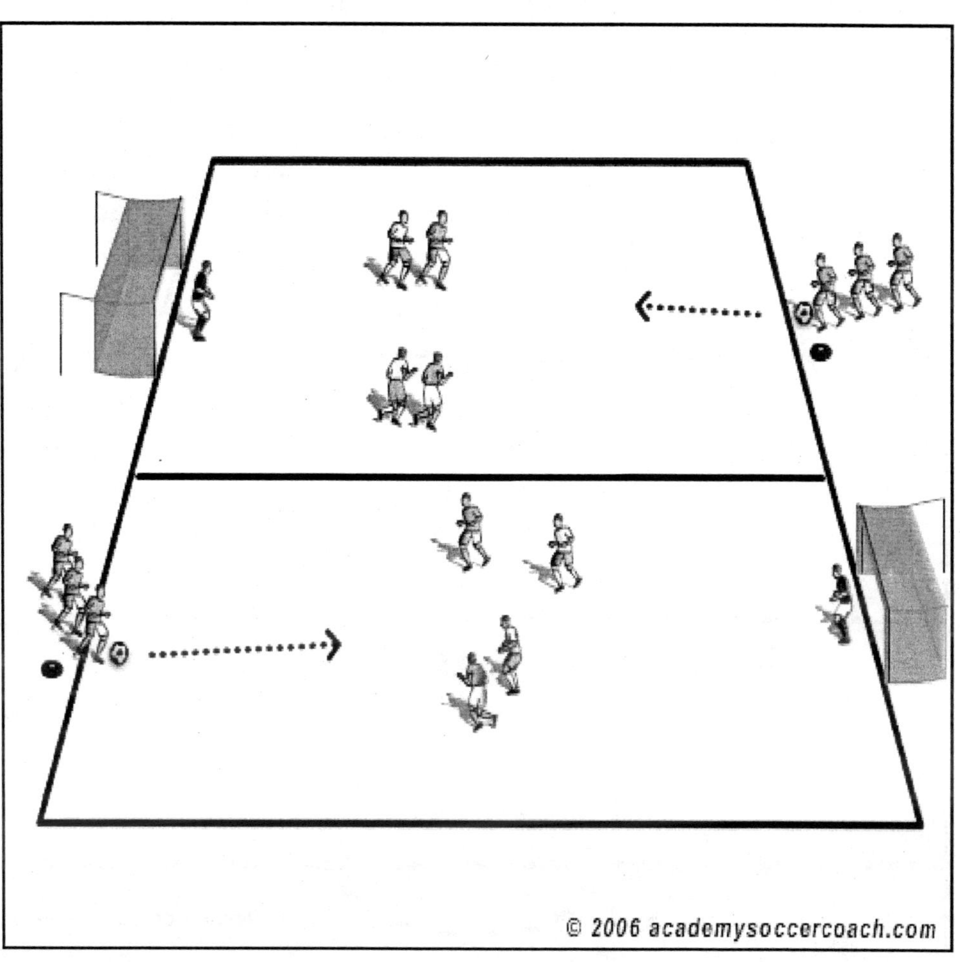

Practice 92

This practice is a progression of the previous practice and includes two defenders
This time the waiting player must dribble onto the pitch and make a 3v2 with the two forwards.

Can the forwards combine and get a shot at goal?

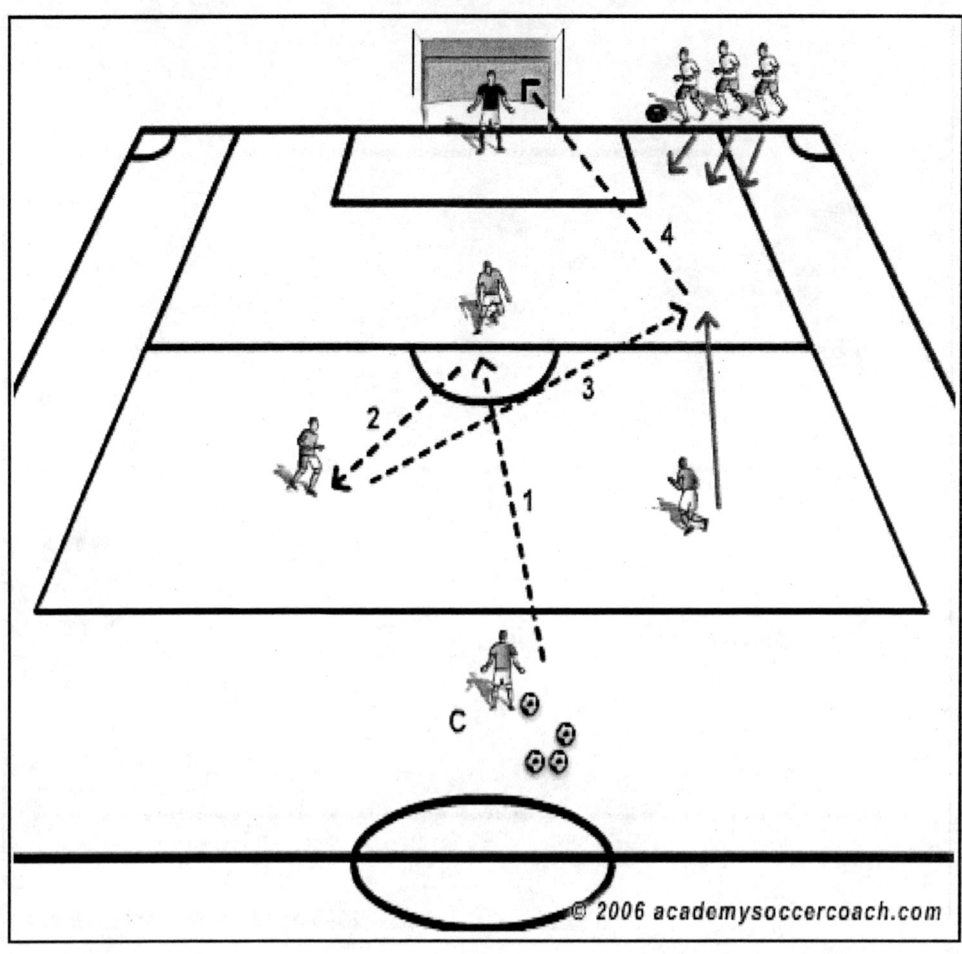

Practice 93

The coach passes a ball into the three forwards who must combine in order to shoot at goal
Once this ball is played, a defender races onto the pitch
The coach now passes a new ball into the forwards who must combine 3v1 to shoot at goal
This sequence continues until a 3v3 is played

The forwards count the number of goals scored and then rotate with the defenders for the next game

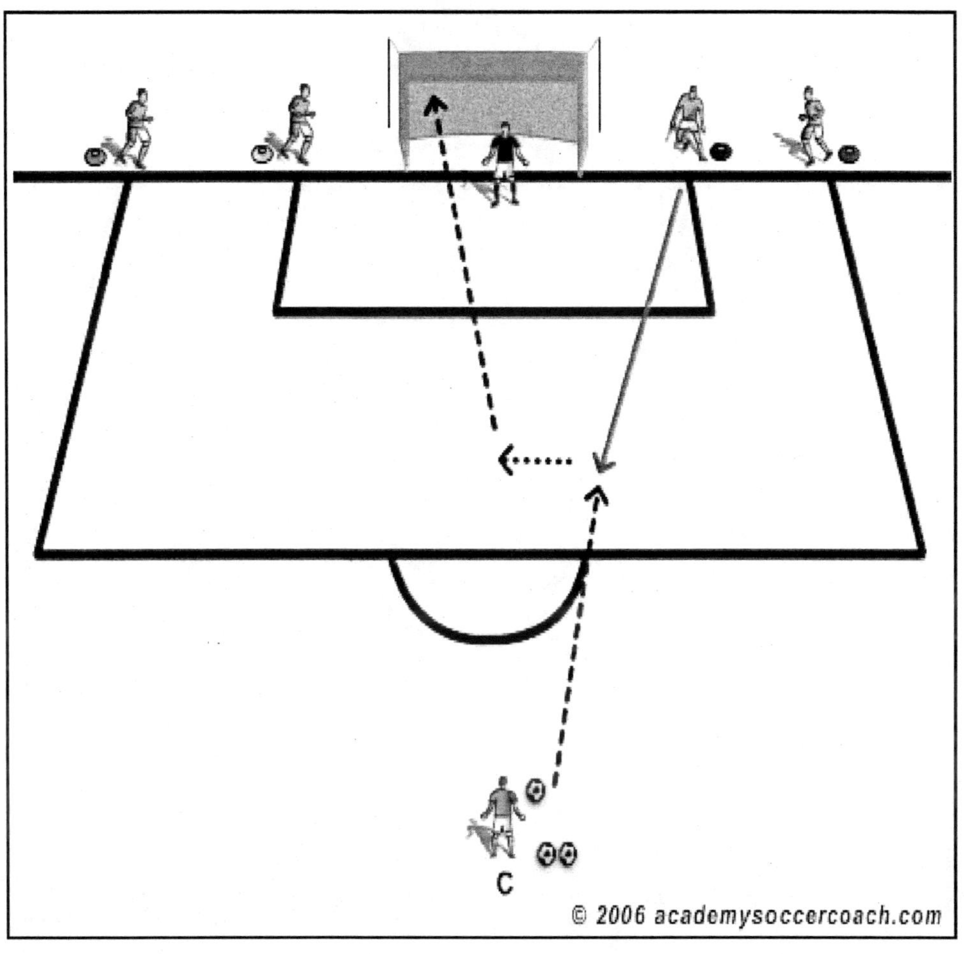

Practice 94

The coach calls the name of the player or color of the cone.
The player called must run to receive a pass from the coach
The player is allowed one touch to turn and one touch to shoot on goal

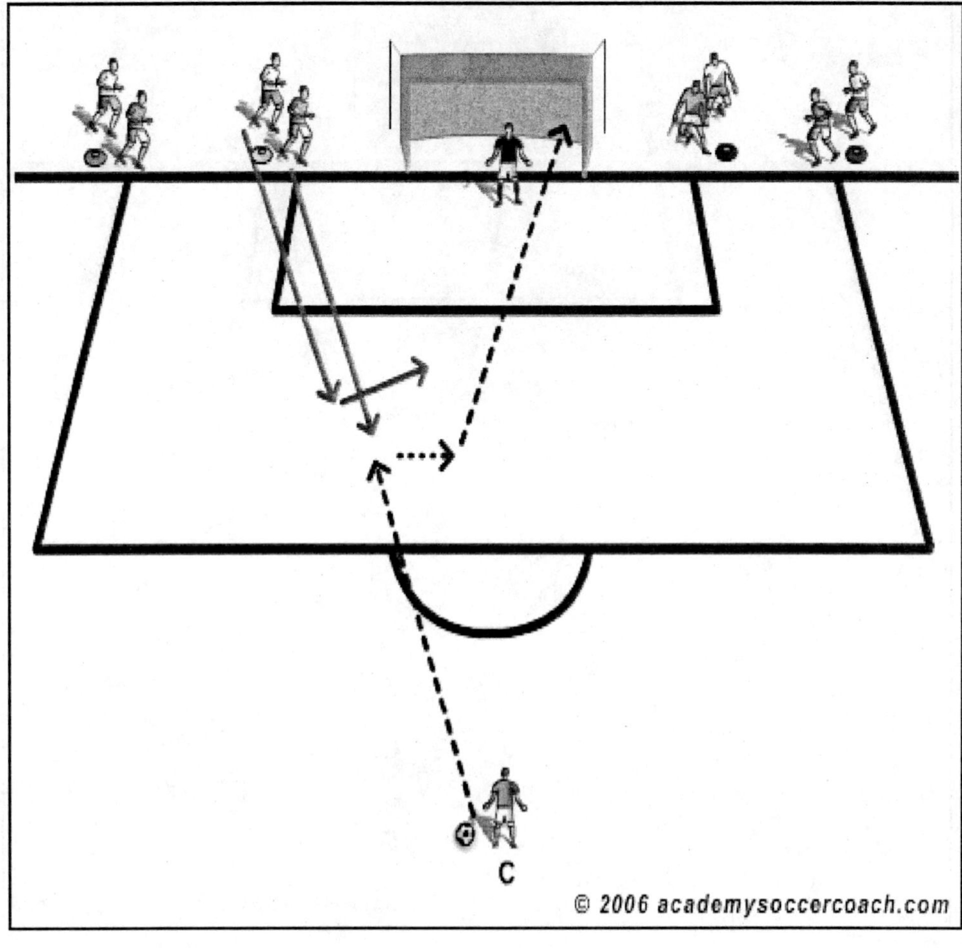

Practice 95

The practice is a progression from practice 94

The coach calls the name of the player or color cone
The player called must run out to receive a pass from the coach
The defender must now run out and stop the attacker from turning to shoot

The attacker and defender rotates positions for the next turn

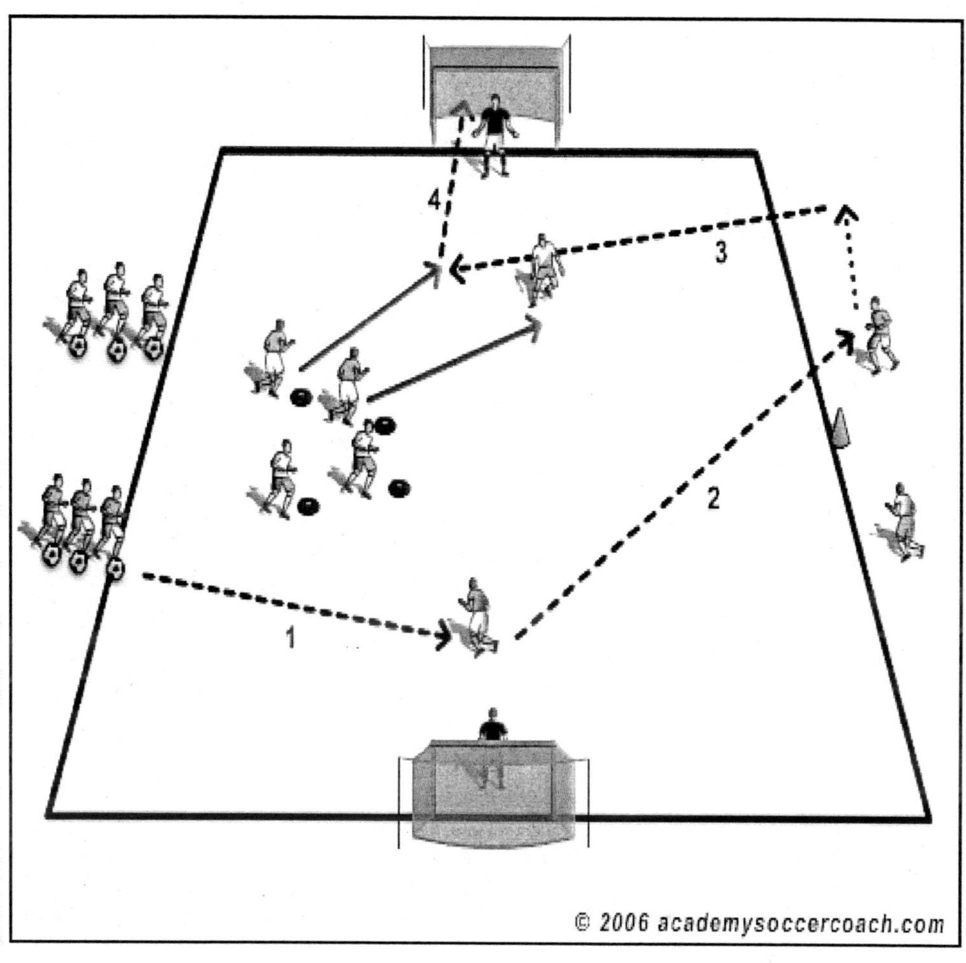

Practice 96

This practice is a right v left footed crossing game

To start, the grey team pass into the central player
The central player passes wide to the crosser
The crosser now crosses for the two forwards who attempt to lose the defender and score.

All players move to the next position on the circuit

Immediately after this ball is played. The practice continues in the opposite direction with the white team now attacking

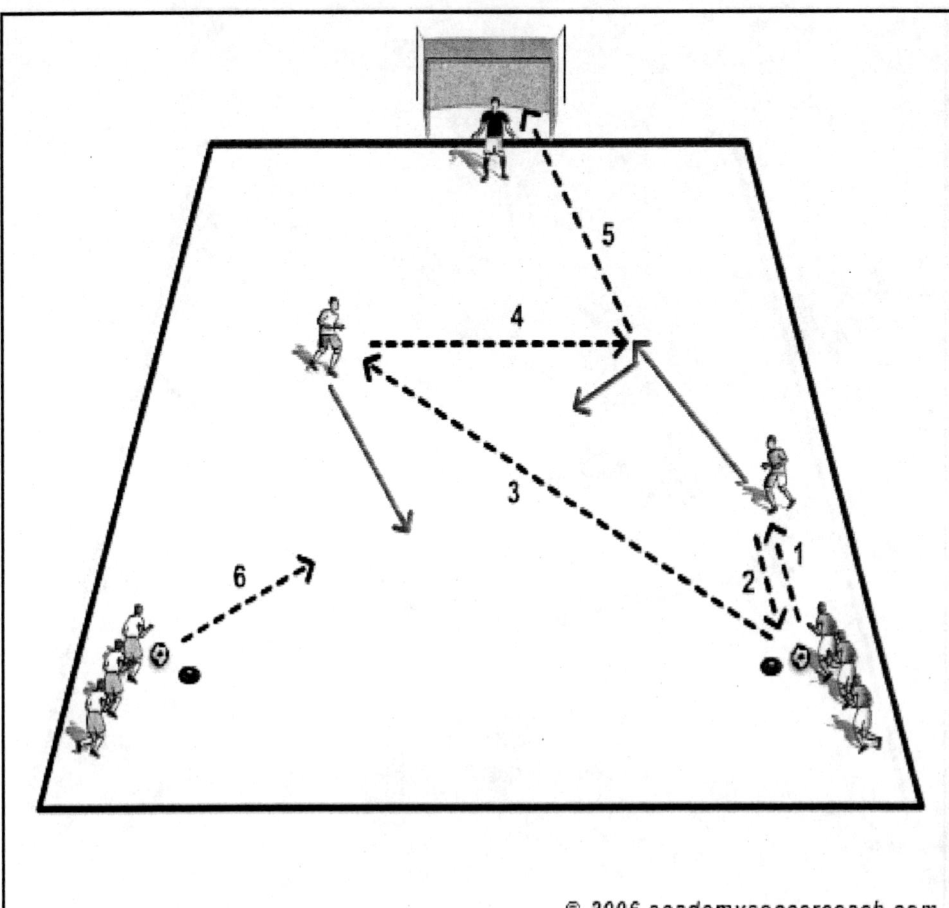

Practice 97

The grey striker comes short and plays a one-two with his team mate.
Now a longer pass is made into the white striker.
The white striker sets the grey striker to shoot at goal
Immediately both players react
The white players calls for a pass from his teammate
The white player dummies this pass and spins to receive a lay off from the grey striker
The white striker now shoots at goal

This practice enables both strikers to combine in order to shoot at goal

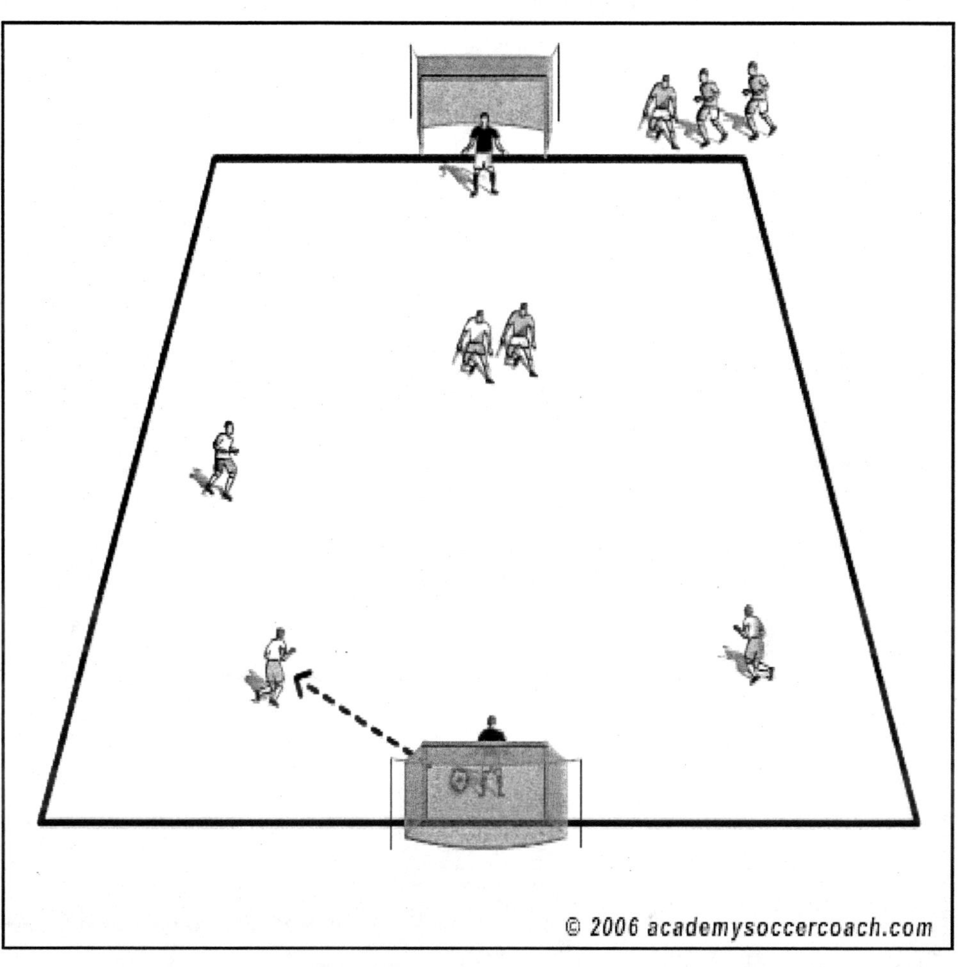

Practice 98

The keeper throws out to the four attackers who must quickly combine and score in a 4v1 situation.
Now a 2nd defender enters the pitch
The keeper throws out to the four attackers and a 4v2 commences
This continues until a 4v4 game is being played
The game continues for a set time period
For the next game, the roles are reversed.

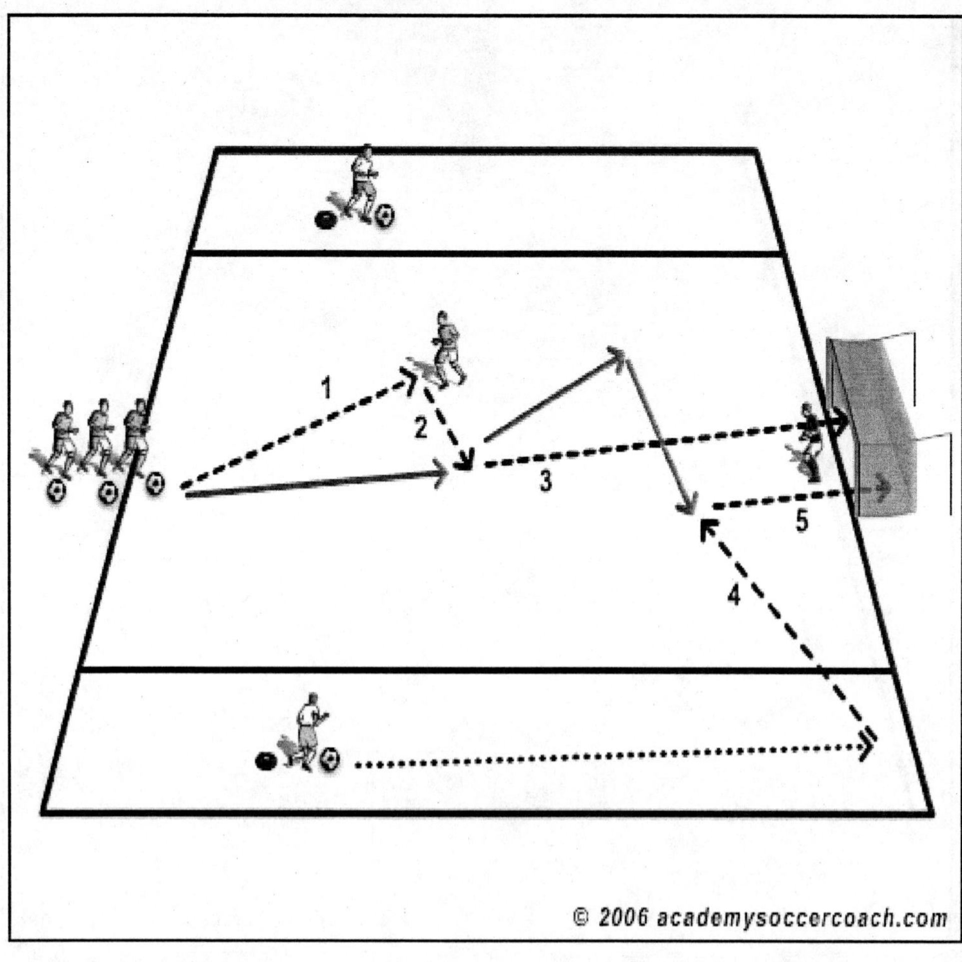

Practice 99

The midfielder plays a pass into the forward and runs to receive a lay off
The midfielder shoots at goal
Immediately, one of the wide players dribbles to cross
The midfielder must now react and attempt to score off the cross

For the next attack, the midfielder becomes the forward

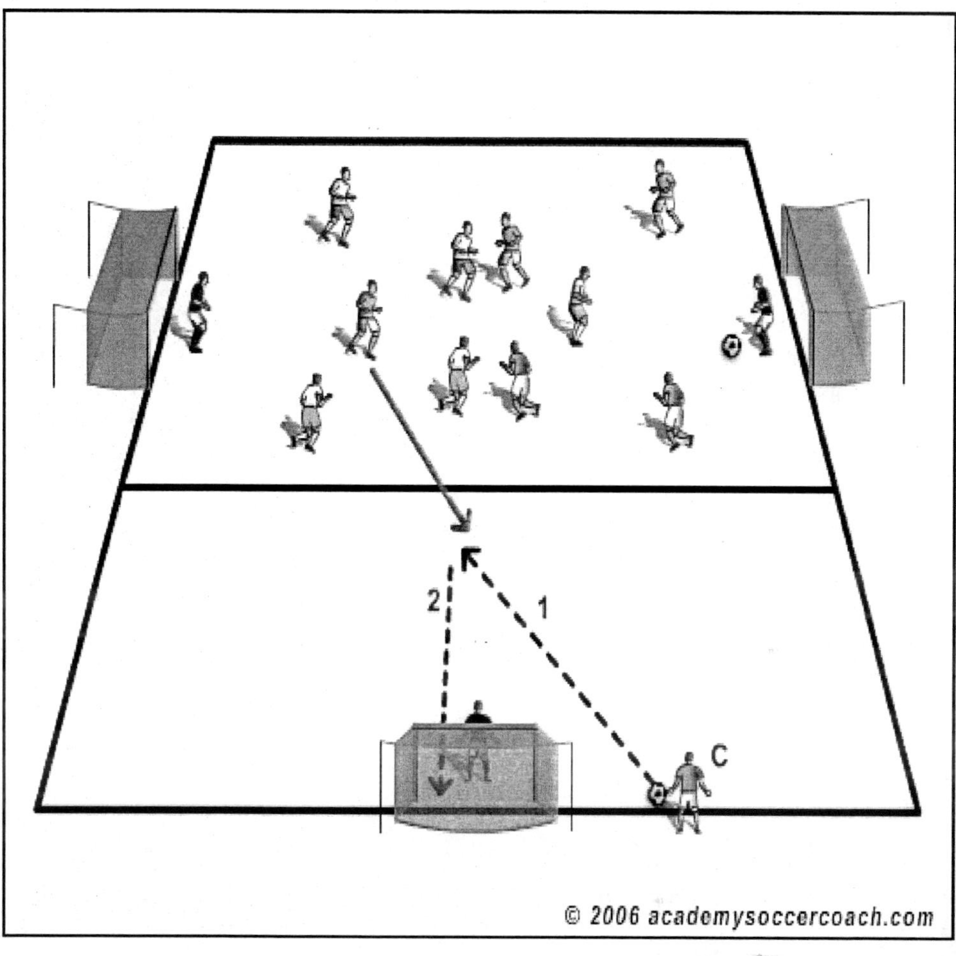

<u>Practice 100</u>

Three goalkeepers
Two teams
One team is numbered with evens
One team is numbered with odds
A normal game is played on the top pitch
On the coaches call of a number, the player called must break out of the pitch
The player now receives a pass from the coach in order to shoot at goal

The player must now race back to the pitch as quick as possible.
The game continues stop and therefore when breaking out to shoot, your team is a player down

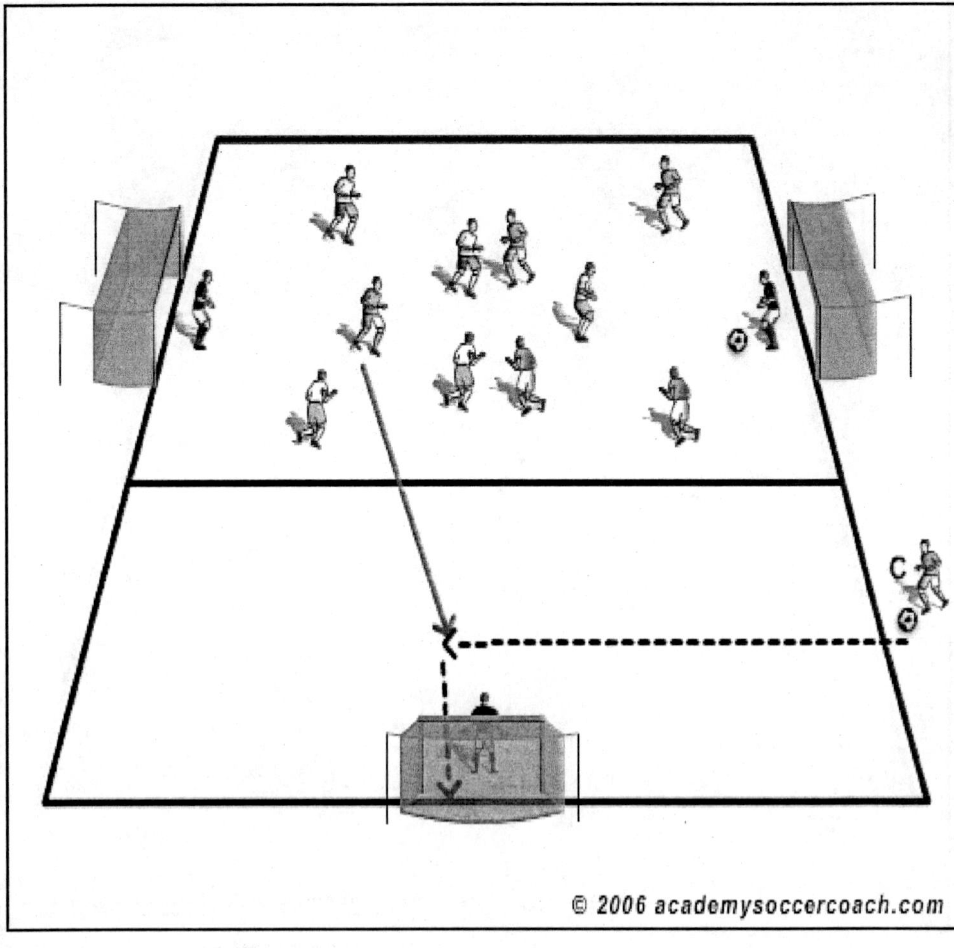

Practice 101

Three goalkeepers
Two teams
One team is numbered with evens
One team is numbered with odds
A normal game is played on the top pitch
On the coaches call of a number, the player called must break out of the pitch
The player receives a cross from the coach in order to shoot at goal

The player must now race back to the pitch as quick as possible.
The game continues stop and therefore when breaking out to shoot, your team is a player down

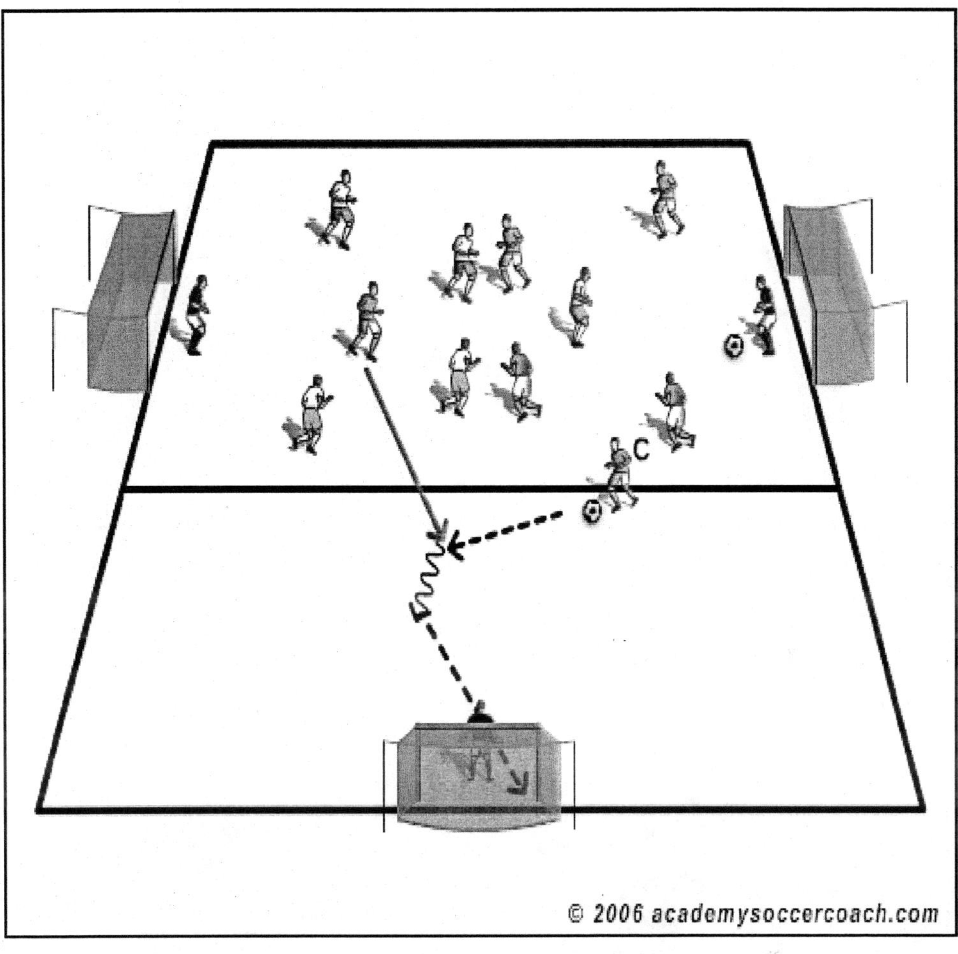

Practice 102

Three goalkeepers
Two teams
One team is numbered with evens
One team is numbered with odds
A normal game is played on the top pitch
On the coaches call of a number, the player called must break out of the pitch
The player receives a ball from the coach in order to dribble and shoot at goal

The player must now race back to the pitch as quick as possible.
The game continues stop and therefore when breaking out to shoot, your team is a player down

Practice 103

This practice is a progression to practice 102

After dribbling to shoot, the players now stay on the pitch as a defender now when a player breaks out to receive a pass from the coach A 1v1 game commences.

Conclusion

I hope the practices in this book will aid you in your careers as soccer coaches.

it is important to inspire your players with the practices you design but all coaches must remember that it is equally important to inspire the players with your individual personality. This cannot be learned on a coaching course, it comes from within.

The way you communicate the session combined with positive body language and bundles of enthusiasm are the keys to developing confident and happy players.

In all walks of life, enthusiasm often outweighs ability. the special people have both of these qualities.

Please feel free to contact me personally with your questions or feedback to my personal address – mbeale4980@aol.com

Best wishes and good luck

Michael Beale